CLIMB
A GUIDE TO HIGH ADVENTURE

Jacob D Nuttall

NAKED SNAIL

BOOKS

© Jacob D Nuttall 2023

All rights reserved. No part of this publication may be produced or transmitted in any form or by any means, electronic or mechanical, including photocopy, recording, or any information storage and retrieval system, without the written permission of the author.

 Jacobdnuttall@outlook.com
 climb_aguidetohighadventure

All content, including design and illustrations, by Jacob D Nuttall.

Please note that the author cannot accept responsibility for any error or omission, or any loss, damage, injury, adverse outcome, or liability of any kind that may result from the use of any of the techniques, instructions, or information contained in this publication or reliance on it. If ever in doubt climbers are advised to seek the guidance of a qualified instructor.

CONTENTS

Introduction		4
Chapter 1	"To climb, or not to climb, that is the question".	6
Chapter 2	All the gear and no idea - Essential kit.	17
Chapter 3	Under cover climber - Climbing in a rock gym.	26
Chapter 4	Hold on... what? - Climbing wall features.	41
Chapter 5	You're not climbing a ladder - Essential technique.	50
Chapter 6	Best foot forwards - The importance of footwork.	55
Chapter 7	Moving on up - Gravity, body position, and movement.	63
Chapter 8	The good, the bad, and the ugly - More on technique.	71
Chapter 9	I'll show you the ropes - A guide to top rope climbing indoors.	80
Chapter 10	Equipped for success - More essential kit.	101
Chapter 11	The Great Outdoors? - Taking the first steps climbing outdoors.	112
Chapter 12	In deep water - Deep Water Soloing/Psicobloc.	129
Chapter 13	It ain't just brawn knucklehead! - Intelligent training.	136
Chapter 14	Climbing is not a competition... unless it is a competition.	159
Acknowledgements		174
Appendix A	Approximate conversion chart of commonly used bouldering grades in Europe and the USA.	176
Appendix B	Approximate conversion chart of commonly used sport climbing grades in Europe and the USA.	177
Index		178

INTRODUCTION

This is a short overview of how I started climbing and why reading this book will help you on your own pathway to becoming a great climber:

A few years back I began meeting up with a buddy and the pair of us would climb for a couple of hours a week at an indoor climbing gym close to our respective homes. Now, when I say "climb", I use the term rather loosely. Back then I climbed much in the same way I imagine the first prehistoric fish dragged itself onto land 400 million years ago – wheezing and puffing, straining every muscle and sinew in its body, moving barely a fraction at a time. And I bet it didn't ache as much as I did the next morning! Here's the thing though - I'm certain that when that prehistoric fish finally dragged itself onto land it felt some sense of achievement for completing its mammoth task... well, maybe not the same kind as you and I, given that it would have had a rudimentary brain stem rather than a brain... but you catch my drift? Similarly(ish), each time I managed to heave, lug, and haul my body to the top of the climbing wall I too felt a sense of achievement. Week by week the pair of us progressed onto harder and harder climbs and our confidence grew exponentially.

When you take up any sport seriously, you quickly begin to realise that there is a lot more to learn than you might have imagined. Much as football isn't just 'kicking a ball', there is a lot more to climbing than just 'scrambling up a wall'. It requires technique, stamina, strength, and the right frame of mind. Indoor climbing gyms are inherently friendly places, so we met a lot of like-minded individuals keen to give tips on how to improve. We sucked up the advice like sponges (and I'm not talking about prehistoric sea sponges), but it didn't stop us from making several silly mistakes – like failing to warm up or stretch properly and overexerting ourselves on difficult climbs. This inevitably led to injury: I quickly developed tendonitis in my elbow and my friend badly sprained his neck (I mean, who even sprains their neck?!).

I also did what I suspect AT LEAST 50% of new climbers do – I bought the wrong equipment. Now, given that for indoor climbing you only actually need a pair of climbing shoes, you would have thought getting this bit right would be an essential move in the grand scheme of things. Wearing a canoe on each foot would have been preferable to the first pair I purchased. My second pair weren't much better: They were so tight they would only realistically have suited Roald Dahl's Witches (they had no toes if you missed my point!). If only I'd had one simple source of information explaining all the fundamental requirements to enable me to progress and develop into a competent and well-rounded climber ... perhaps a book written by someone who'd made all the mistakes?

Well, it didn't stop there... A year into my own climbing journey, it dawned on me that if my kids (Amelie, aged 10 and Florence, aged 7) started climbing, it would provide ample ~~excuse~~ reason for me to get to a climbing wall more regularly. And so, I 'selflessly' enrolled them onto a dedicated climbing course, and later, a climbing squad; guaranteeing they would develop as climbers and, of course, so I could live my own dreams vicariously through them! Finally, assured that I had the moral highground, I encouraged my wife along, the declaration, "We could go climbing as a family!" ringing in her ears.

I guess you might be thinking, "Surely there'd be NOTHING WORSE than having your parents around when you're learning new skills and meeting new friends?" Turns out, you're spot on. As I had a bit of climbing experience, I tried to give them advice on climbing technique. Apparently, sighing loudly, raising one's eyebrows, and starting sentences like, "Don't do it like that..." or, "Get a move on..." aren't conducive to a positive learning environment. It took a few skirmishes before I finally took the hint. All climbers find themselves in a position out of their comfort zone and it is at that exact point they need POSITIVE ENCOURAGEMENT. Having the right mindset will help you climb higher and better than you could ever have imagined.

As well as my questionable input, the kids received climbing specific training from experienced coaches, requiring them to apply newly learnt techniques, train to improve deficiencies, and understand the impact that regular climbing was having on their bodies. They entered competitions and, along with trying to get to grips with the mind-boggling rules and regulations, had to deal with the psychological impact of success and failure. The road was occasionally bumpy and, the continuing theme along the way was, we still made mistakes! This included packing insufficient food for a whole day's climbing, and arriving at the allocated start time for a climbing competition... What? Yes, I did say, "arriving at the allocated start time" (always arrive at least an hour early to register and warm up ...WHO KNEW?!).

Suffice to say, the aim of this book is to help you navigate safely and confidently into rock climbing, avoiding some of the pitfalls that arose along our own path of understanding. This book follows the same path that I took, one of the most common routes into climbing these days: beginning in the setting of an indoor climbing gym where I (eventually!) learnt key techniques to make my climbing more safe, efficient, and ultimately more enjoyable, before venturing outdoors and into competition. It includes some basic training plans to make your body better able to tolerate the stresses and strains of climbing, and a load of other climbing related 'stuff' that will make life A LOT easier in the long term.

1

"TO CLIMB, OR NOT TO CLIMB, THAT IS THE QUESTION"

> This chapter will help you understand:
>
> - The reasons to get involved in climbing.
> - That there will be some place nearby you can do it.
> - The different types of climbing available to you.
> - The fact that anyone can learn to climb!

But seriously... why climb?

What's the point? It's a valid question, isn't it? I mean, why do hundreds of thousands of people engage in an activity that involves clambering up a wall or rock face one moment, only to come back down again shortly afterwards? It sounds a bit daft when put in those simplistic terms. But it's only daft in the same way that lots of people right now are chasing a leather ball around a field, balancing on a piece of fibreglass on top of a wave, or running around a rubber track as fast as they can.

George Mallory was a British mountaineer and climber who made several expeditions to Everest in the 1920's. When asked by a reporter for the New York Times why he wanted to climb Mount Everest, he replied, "Because it's there..."

I tried to impress upon a young child the existential importance of such a quote when he shouted, "Why are you climbing that?" whilst I was attempting to scale a rock face in Southeast England one fine sunny day. "Because it's there..." I replied knowingly. He immediately turned to his parents and spat, "That's just stupid!" and wandered off in the other direction. Had I been quick, I might have followed up with more of Mallory's insight:

"Its existence is a challenge. The answer is instinctive, a part I suppose, of man's desire to conquer the universe."

However, by then he had gone and all I could do was mutter, "Little twerp!" under my breath as I reached for the next hold.

On reflection, perhaps I should have tried harder: I could have clambered down the rock face, chased after him and explained that climbing is exhilarating, sociable, and really good fun. Had this grasped his attention, I would have continued, outlining how climbing involves the development of strength and mobility of the body including the fingers, hands, arms, shoulders, core, thighs, calves, feet, and toes as well as fine tuning cognitive skills such as hand-eye coordination and spatial awareness. Finally, I would round off with the fact that climbing encourages problem solving, decision making, concentration, focused communication, and even the development of new language skills such as, "WHOA DUDE, you totally CRUSHED that!"

So why climb? With so much to gain, why wouldn't you?!

Where to climb?

So now you know why you should climb, it's key that you also discover where you can go to do it! There are two main choices:

(i)   An **artificial** climbing wall.
(ii)   A **natural** rock face, cliff, or boulder.

Climbing on an artificial climbing wall is usually done at a climbing gym. Although some climbing gyms have outdoor walls, the vast majority are located indoors (i.e. under cover). For the uninitiated, a climbing gym usually consists of a warehouse with interior walls covered in multicoloured holds. The holds are arranged in such a way that the pathway, or route, on which a climber can reach the top is different on each occasion. People pay to go in and climb up the different routes. Seems bizarre now I read it back, but it really isn't much more complicated than that (and if it does sound complicated, then you're going to have to concentrate really hard for the rest of this book).

The main benefit of climbing gyms is that they are managed environments: there will be staff on standby to assist, guide or instruct you depending on your experience and requirements. You can generally be assured that everything you climb has been rigidly safety tested, including the walls themselves (i.e. they're not going to collapse, or bits drop off onto your head), and any equipment you might require will have been subject to regular inspection.

In contrast, climbing on a natural rock face will invariably be outdoors and, unless you have specifically arranged instruction, unsupervised. Although the mechanics of climbing are essentially the same, rock climbing on 'real' rock outdoors brings with it additional variables, not least the weather, wildlife, and the fact that there aren't any obvious, multicoloured holds to follow! If you are new to climbing or have only climbed indoors on artificial rock, then I wouldn't advise transitioning to the 'great outdoors' unless you are accompanied by an experienced climber, coach, or guide (I explore the different challenges posed by outdoor climbing in Chapter 11).

Establishing exactly where to climb is the easy bit. There are a GAZILION apps, blogs, posts, mags, and books detailing climbing locations all over the world. You may be lucky enough to live in an area where there are natural rocky outcrops suitable for climbing, or you might find there is nothing for miles. Fortunately, climbing gyms are becoming an increasingly popular alternative to the standard mechanical weights and running machine type set-up, with multiple such establishments springing up anywhere and everywhere. You just need to search what's available near you and work from there.

Types of climbing

There are lots of different types of climbing which can be undertaken indoors, outdoors, or both. Climbing can be loosely categorised into two groups: **ROPE** and **NON-ROPE** climbing.

Rope climbing is basically climbing with a rope connected to the climber to prevent injury in the event of a fall. Non-rope climbing is climbing without a rope (I bet you knew that before your read it... See, you already know more than you realised!). Just to be clear: climbing without a rope doesn't necessarily mean it's going to be more dangerous, although it can be... Confused? Let's take a brief look at the most common types of climbing and hopefully things will become clearer.

Non-rope climbing

Bouldering (indoor or outdoor)

A 'boulder' is a detached fragment of rock. In bouldering, climbers ascend or traverse a short route on a real, or artificial, boulder. The concept is about as straight forward as it gets: get from the hold at the start of the route to either the last hold (indoors) or top of the boulder (outdoors) in one continuous go, without falling off. I know you might be thinking, "Well DUH! Of course, I don't want to FALL OFF because I don't want to DIE!!!" It's okay... generally bouldering routes don't tend to be more than a few metres high, and most boulderers rely on soft matting to help break any fall.

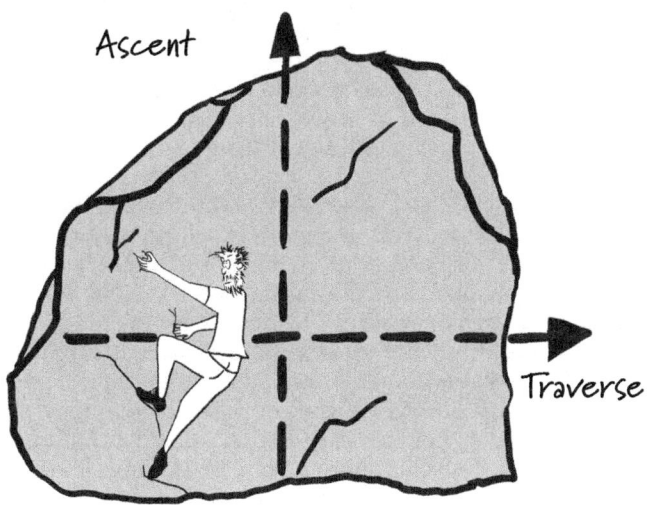

In fact, a geologist would tell you that a boulder can be any rock fragment with a diameter greater than 256 millimetres! But, just to be clear, bouldering involves climbing somewhat larger boulders (unless your name happens to be Gulliver and you're on vacation).

Bouldering was originally regarded as a means of training for much longer rope climbs, with a key focus on the development of technique, strength, and power. However, it has since become recognised as a form of climbing in its own right. In fact, its popularity has EXPLODED, with many climbing gyms popping up, exclusively for bouldering. Why?

Well, it's probably the easiest and most accessible route into climbing: You don't need any technical equipment other than a pair of shoes especially made for climbing (Guess what they're called? Yes, that's it – CLIMBING SHOES!) and can pretty much get started after a safety briefing and introduction to the basics.

Climbing gyms are jam-packed with short climbing routes, each designated by a tag or different coloured holds. The obvious markings make it clear what holds are 'in play' so that you don't just scramble all over the place willy-nilly. Additionally, bouldering gyms are decked out with soft matting to help prevent injury from a fall.

In contrast, outdoor bouldering requires the climber to work out how to ascend a particular section of rock using available features. Climbers must rely on any matting that they bring with them to break a fall.

Deep Water Soloing (DWS) (Outdoor climbing above water)

If you didn't have any soft matting to break your fall then the next best thing to fall on (or in) is… water, or DEEP WATER to be more precise. Whilst you occasionally may find an artificial climbing wall purposefully built over a swimming pool, DWS, otherwise known as PSICOBLOC, is normally practiced on sea cliffs where a fall will, or at least should, be into a pool of water deep enough that the climber doesn't hit the bottom.

Think of it: sun, sea, sand, and your NEW favourite pastime… climbing! What couldn't be more perfect? Well, for starters, climbing on the coast requires a lot more planning and preparation than you might realise. For instance, depending on the time of year and location, sea water can be F-R-E-E-Z-I-N-G; plus, climbers need to take account of tide conditions (the height and time of water changes throughout the month). You wouldn't want to find yourself stuck on a cove that has become cut off due to a rising tide, or climbing over water that was 10 metres deeper earlier in the day but only 1 metre when you begin your climb. Nevertheless, Deep Water Soloing can be fantastic fun and is a relatively 'free' style of climbing, the only real requirements being a pair of climbing shoes and a willingness to get wet!

Free Solo (Outdoor climbing at great height)

Free soloing involves climbing completely unaided… No rope, no harness, no soft landing, no protection. I would add… no mistakes, no second chances, and no insurance. Some people consider free soloing as the 'purest' form of climbing (although you could also argue that climbing in its purest form would be climbing without any climbing shoes or clothes at all… I have no doubt that somewhere on the internet there is a place for naked rock climbing, but just think of the rock chaff!). Sadly, numerous skilled rock climbers have died whilst free soloing because it only takes one tiny error – a slip on a foot or hand hold - could turn the tables between life and death.

Rope climbing

In general, most people climbing any higher than a few metres will do so with the additional safety benefit of a rope. One end of rope will be attached to...

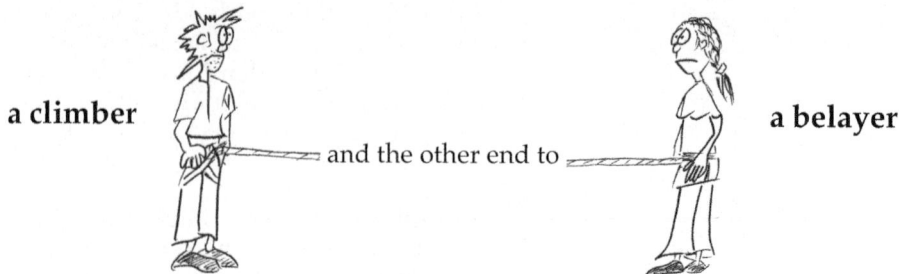

a climber and the other end to **a belayer**

That's not all… otherwise your set up won't really add much to safety! The rope is attached to the wall or rock face that is being climbed so that, if a climber falls, they will be held on the wall by the rope rather than landing on the floor.

Top rope climbing (indoors or outdoors)

'Top roping' is the simplest form of rope climbing where the rope runs through an anchor at the TOP of the route. The 'anchor' is the point of attachment between the wall and the rope. As the climber climbs, the belayer pulls the slack rope through the anchor. If the climber fell, the belayer will effectively 'put on the brakes' so that the climber would only travel a very short distance.

You may have picked up already... being a belayer is a really, really important role. Personally, I think belayer sounds a bit lame but, 'the person who is effectively in charge of your life' is probably a bit too much of a mouthful.

Sport climbing (Indoor or outdoor climbing on preset routes)

Like top roping, sport or 'lead' climbing involves being tied to one end of a rope, with a belayer on the other. However, to sport climb, you need someone to have drilled holes in the wall you intend to climb and placed bolts along the route (these are bolts especially adapted for climbing - unlikely to be the same ones in the bottom of your old man's DIY toolkit). A climber ascends the wall whilst clipping their rope into a series of 'quickdraws', pieces of equipment that are attached to each bolt.

Indoor climbing gyms generally have bolted routes with quickdraws already attached, but outdoors, climbers need to carry and affix their own quickdraws to the bolted route. There is quite a lot more to mentally prepare for when sport climbing because the act of clipping a rope is an art form. If a climber misses a clip and falls, they will fall past the quickdraw they tried to clip as well as the last one they successfully clipped, and sometimes that can be a very long way!

Trad Climbing (outdoor climbing using protective gear)

Trad, short for 'traditional' climbing, involves leading up a route, but rather than clipping rope into fixed bolts, the climber places their own protective equipment along the way. They're essentially fixing temporary bolts in the rock face that will hold their weight in the event of a fall. A trad climber not only needs to carry enough protective equipment to get them up a route, but they also need to be skilled at placing it effectively, because if it isn't secure, it could 'pop out' in the event the climber fell, the consequences of which could be disastrous. As such, trad climbers carry a bewildering variety of 'protection', including cams, nuts, hexes, tricams and slings to name a few; the correct placement of which could form the basis of a book in their own right! As if that wasn't enough, once the protective gear has been used, it needs to be removed (otherwise trad climbing would be a very, very expensive pursuit), usually as the climber ascends the route.

Whereas a sports climber is limited to established, bolted routes, the ability to effectively create your own climbing route provides total freedom for a trad climber to climb anywhere they like, with the added benefit that little or no damage is caused to the rock face.

Trad climbing is where you might hear the term BIG WALL climbing; and I'm not just talking Berlin Wall big (albeit it got knocked down) or the Great Wall of China big… I'm talking COLOSSAL. These 'walls' are so big they require days, even weeks to climb using multiple 'pitches' where climbers have got to live on the wall!

To put it in perspective, your average indoor climbing wall is anywhere between 10-20 metres high, whereas El Capitan, Yosemite, USA is over 1000 metres high, and there isn't a coffee shop in sight.

Speed Climbing (Indoor or outdoor fast paced climbing on an artificial wall)

Basically, a vertical sprint. What's the aim? Seriously? Do you really have to ask? Well, the clue's in the title - speed. It's simply about who gets to the top fastest. Speed climbing is very much competition focused, and there's not too much to know:

The walls are ALWAYS 15 metres high, hanging at a 5-degree angle.

The holds are IDENTICAL and placed EXACTLY in the same order.

Climbers race side by side, secured by an auto-belay (like an automatic security rope).

Time starts when there is a loud "BEEP!"

Time stops when you strike a button at the end of the route.

That's it... Bomb up the wall like you're being chased by a mad axeman!!!

Well, that would be fine as long as the 'mad axeman' isn't one of the current world record holders who have scaled the 15 metres wall in under 6 seconds. I can barely touch my toes in that time!!!

If you're good at the sprint, then make sure your training includes running directly up a wall…

- 12 -

Ice Climbing (indoor or outdoor climbing on ice)

If you're anything like me, the only experience you have with ICE is (a) slipping on your butt in the winter or (b) sticking some cubes in your drink in the summer. But climbing in sub-zero conditions is very much 'A THING'. Ordinarily, an ice climber would ascend something like a frozen waterfall, or a cliff covered in ice, although there are some indoor ice climbing venues.

Like rock climbing, ice climbers use a rope and harness to ascend an ice wall. An ice climber will be equipped with items that can pierce the ice and gain purchase to move in an upward direction. To an outsider, they probably look more like they are about to engage in medieval battle than ascend a wall. Kit includes an ice axe (for each hand) and sharp metal boot attachments, called crampons.

Although sometimes scary, falling in rock climbing can be relatively common, particularly if a climber is trying to defeat a difficult route. Consider falling with a pair of blades attached to your feet and an axe in each hand!!! Rope doesn't like sharp items and nor do body parts! As such, ice climbers do their utmost NOT to fall.

Unlike 'ordinary' rock climbing, assessing the difficulty of an ice climb can be difficult. Whereas a rock face will barely change over years, the features of an ice climb can change with the seasons. A sport for the fearless and those who prefer the cold!

What does a 'climber' look like?

Many people associate a 'rock climber' as someone who is either (1) fearless or (2) completely bonkers (or a combination of the two). Dangling on the end of a rope off the side of a cliff mightn't sound hugely appealing, especially when you add in the possibility of something horrific happening, like the rope snapping or a rock falling on your head! In fact, just the thought of being high off the ground is enough to put a lot of people off. Acrophobia, the fear of heights, is one of the most common phobias in the world, so its perhaps surprising that climbing is becoming such a popular pastime. So, let's get one thing straight from the start: you don't have to scale a cliff, hold onto the edge of a building by your fingertips or dangle off the end of a rope to get into rock climbing. Well... you can if you really want to, but it's certainly not a prerequisite to becoming a good climber.

Some people get 'butterflies' in their stomach when they are about to try something radically new. I get giant, crazed Pterodactyls GOING MENTAL in mine! So, when I look back, I realise I was asked if I wanted to go climbing a few times in my life and, on every occasion, there was some reason or half reason why I couldn't make it. It took me YEARS to finally sum up the energy and courage to say, "Yep, okay!" To this day I KICK MYSELF that I let doubt, nerves, and just plain lethargy get in the way of discovering something that is now my PASSION.

My friend was the same when I threatened to take him to a climbing gym. He said, "Whoa! Won't catch me climbing! I'm so fat I'd probably pull the wall down!" I finally dragged him, kicking, and screaming, to an indoor climbing wall: FACT 1 – he did not pull the climbing wall down. FACT 2 - If he had managed to pull the wall down, I'd have been super impressed #Incredible Hulk buddy. He **is** a big guy, but do you have to be small to climb? Absolutely NOT... climbers come in all shapes and sizes!

If you look to the animal world to identify 'good climbers', there are some obvious ones, like monkeys, lizards, and spiders... But would you necessarily think of larger, proficient climbers such as the GIANT PANDA?! Giant Pandas weigh up to 160KG and yet they are great tree climbers.

Pandas are a species of BEAR... you know, those giant, hairy things that don't look like they could climb either.... Well, some of them - like the BLACK BEAR - can literally run up a tree. They're so good at climbing, trekkers are often advised NOT to try and climb a tree to get away from them, because they will scale it and STILL EAT YOU!

Still not convinced?

Boo Hoo! - too weak, too fat, too thin, too short, or too scared to climb?
Don't be...
Blind?
Born without a hand?
Shark bit your arm off?
Leg amputee?
Brain damaged in an accident?
Genetic disease?

It need not stop you.

There are plenty of people who enjoy climbing who have a disability, impairment, or are just plain different to 'the norm'. Climbing is a unique sport, and you can ADAPT how you climb to suit your own needs. You can even get a specialist harness and take your wheelchair for a vertical ride if you're that attached to it!

In fact, many ADAPTIVE CLIMBERS are so goddamn good that global organisations such as the International Federation of Sport Climbing (IFSC) has been running paraclimbing competitions for years, with different subcategories to make things fairer! These include:

Category AU: Arm/forearm amputees

Category AL: Leg amputee & paraplegics can use prosthetic limbs

Category B: Visually impaired athletes will climb under the instruction of a 'sight guide', someone who can accurately describe the route and the moves and techniques required to achieve it.

Category RP: Limited range, power, and stability due to neurological impairment (e.g. MS, stroke, brain injury)

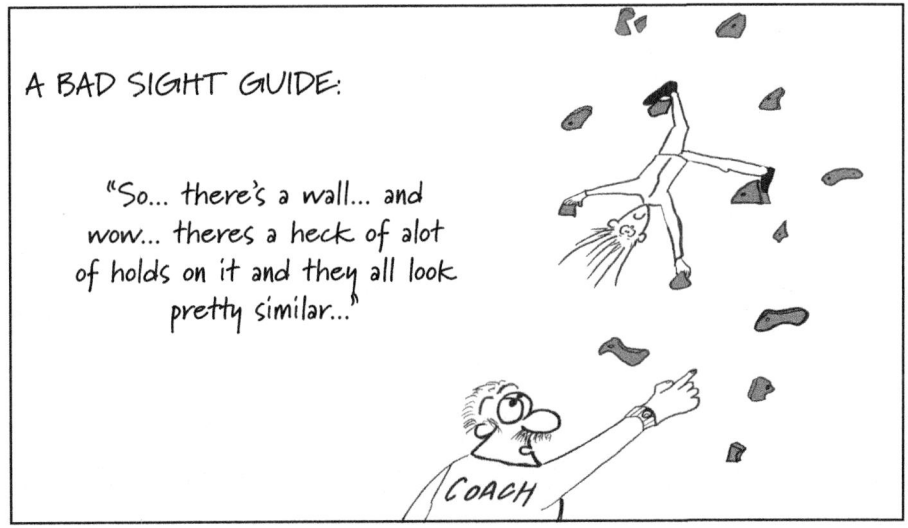

So, you should now realise that a 'climber' needn't be some fearless muscle-bound hulk or a weightless, toned beauty effortlessly scaling cliffs that tower so high they make your stomach churn. I'm sure there are plenty of people like that (particularly if you believe everything you see on Instagram, Tik-Tok, Facebook, Snapchat, and every other social media site containing choreographed shots of posing wanna-be Adonises), but frankly, who cares! Even Peter Parker had to start somewhere... Now I'm not suggesting you try and get a radioactive spider to bite you. But I am saying: even if your IMAGE of a climber doesn't fit with WHO YOU ARE, don't let it stop you giving it a go.

The least you need to know

- Climbing isn't just clambering up a wall. It is an activity that provides physical and mental benefits.

- Climbing can be performed on real or artificial rock, within an indoor or outdoor environment.

- There are various types of climbing, including *non-rope* climbing such as bouldering, deep water soloing (psicobloc), and free solo and *rope* climbing such as top rope, sport (lead), trad, speed, and ice climbing.

- Literally anyone can climb!

2

ALL THE GEAR AND NO IDEA: ESSENTIAL KIT

> Like many sports, you could spend a huge amount of money on a vast array of climbing related STUFF, but at a basic, grass roots level, there are only a couple of items of kit you need to get started - Shoes and chalk. That's literally it! This chapter will:
>
> - Outline the different styles of climbing shoe available and help you choose the right pair.
> - Describe the benefits and drawbacks of different types of chalk.

Climbing shoes

When you are climbing, you are connected to the wall by your hands and feet (as well as occasionally your elbow, knee, butt, or anything else that you need to use to stop you falling off). The surface of your feet, and more specifically, your toes, play a crucial part in balancing on holds or 'smearing' up the surface of the wall itself. Choosing the RIGHT climbing shoe is MEGA important (as is choosing the LEFT climbing shoe – Gettit?!).

Generally, climbing shoes should be a tighter fit than your normal shoes, so that there is absolutely no slippage when you move, and are invariably worn with no socks. I suspect the thought of having to stick your bare foot into a shoe may be the SOLE influencing factor as to whether you choose to go for new or a pre-used pair, but there are a few things to consider…

Hire shoes

If you're going indoor climbing for the first time then it's probably worthwhile hiring shoes, just until you establish whether climbing is something you'd like to pursue further. Similarly, if money is an issue or you're not planning on going climbing that often, then hiring may well be the most cost-effective option. A pair of reasonably good climbing shoes can be costly, whereas MOST climbing gyms provide hire shoes for a fraction of the price. Depends how big your pockets are.

Some hire shoes can be pretty good quality and, if the staff are any good, they will check that they properly fit you. The only drawback is that hire shoes will have been worn before… perhaps once, twice if you're lucky… but more likely by several people a day / week. That means they're going to be a bit stretched and worn but will have been disinfected post-use (hopefully!).

If you're climbing regularly and paying for hire shoes every time, there comes a point when you might as well bite the bullet and buy a pair.

Second-hand shoes

Second-hand sales of climbing shoes are common. The internet is littered with sellers who have bought a pair of shoes that don't fit, used them a few times and then try and claw back some of their hard-earned cash via an online sale. So, you could pick up a bargain… or you could pick up… Athlete's foot or some other gross FOOT FUNGUS!

"There's not mushroom for improvement…"

Having a quick root around a second-hand sales site I found, there were a few shoes that looked okay, but there were just as many that didn't!

One pair looked so badly worn, chances are they were being sold by 'Wee-Poop-Mac-Plop-Foot' the most rotten-stink-footed climber this side of the Western Hemisphere. And I could have bought brand new for slightly more than their asking price…

YES, you can always clean them up, BUT the most important thing is buying a pair that you know will fit, otherwise you'll have to research, "How to sell second-hand – second-hand shoes" on the internet!

New shoes

Although there is a huge selection of climbing shoes on offer, the only way of guaranteeing a pair that fit, is to go to a reputable shop and, with the help of an expert, try some on. Your challenge, should you choose to accept it, is to find a reputable shop! Just to clarify, I'm not saying, climbing shoes salesmen are disreputable, I'm just saying there aren't that many around! If you're lucky, your local climbing gym will have a selection and, more-often-than-not, the staff will be climbing-mad and therefore likely to understand your requirements. Some of the better outdoor gear shops also stock climbing shoes and may also have some good staff to assist. You'll get a clear steer from the size of the display: if there is a large variety of shoes and the shop assistant starts asking about your climbing experience or what type of climbing you'll be doing, you're off to a good start. If the display amounts to a few dust covered shoes sized extra-large and extra-small, I'd give it a WIDE BERTH.

Remember, although bartering for climbing shoes isn't generally accepted practice, it is worth establishing whether they will PRICE MATCH online offers, which can sometimes be lower.

Types of climbing shoe

Just as there are certain tools for certain jobs, there are different types of climbing shoes for different types of climbing and different levels of experience.

So, the RIGHT climbing shoes aren't necessarily going to be (a) the coolest looking ones in the store, (b) the pair your climbing icon wears, or (c) the pair currently on sale in the bargain bucket! You really need to (HONESTLY) consider what level of climber you are (beginner, intermediate, or professional), as well as what type of climbing you intend to do, because ultimately, you will be relying on them to keep you glued to the wall. There are three basic types:

Neutral

Neutral shoes allow your feet and toes to lie flat in the shoe, making them more comfortable than other climbing shoes. That can be the difference in feel between wearing a pair of slippers and wearing a pair of high heels (or so I'm told)! Neutral shoes also tend to have thicker soles, providing good support, and will last longer. They are great for either beginner climbers, or anyone intending to undertake a long day's climbing.

Aggressive

Aggressive shoes aren't ones with an attitude problem, although they may make you scream in anger trying to put them on. Aggressive shoes are at the opposite end of the spectrum to neutral shoes. They tend to have a very downturned shape and a super snug fit, which make them ideal for difficult overhanging problems. However, although having your toes in a downturned position may assist in focusing power, you'll likely have to take them off repeatedly to give your feet a rest. Aggressive shoes often have thinner soles for maximum sensitivity between the foot and the climbing surface. Good 'footwork' is therefore important as the rubber will wear much quicker.

Moderate

The all-purpose terrain vehicle of climbing shoes, moderate shoes are basically anywhere in the middle between neutral and aggressive: they tend to have a slightly thinner sole than neutral ones, making them a bit more sensitive, and usually slightly downturned for additional power, enabling the climber to ascend a variety of different climbs.

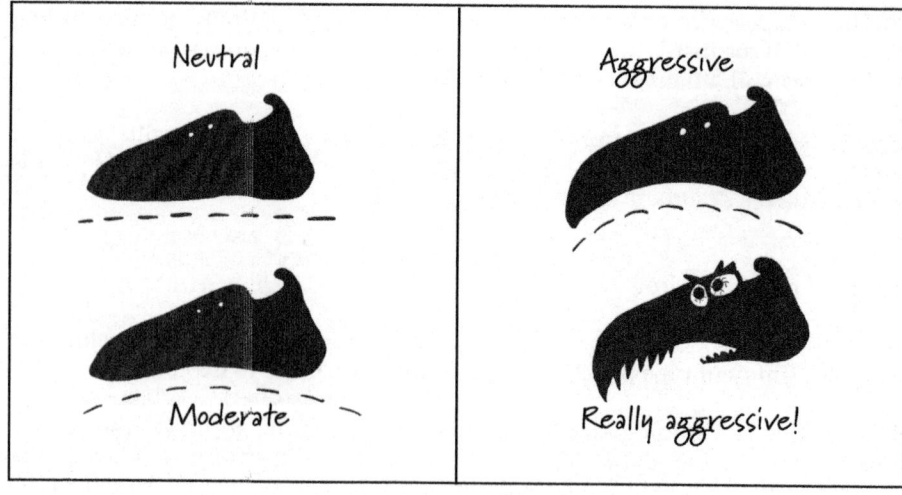

Shoe fitting

Here are some tips to ensure you get a pair of shoes that are right for you:

- When buying a pair of everyday shoes, it is normal practice to stand up and walk around when fitting. Dare I say it: climbing shoes aren't made for walking, so wandering around in them for a couple of minutes isn't necessarily going to be that telling. You should be able to determine the general fit from a sitting position.

- Climbing shoes are meant to be worn with bare feet, to help prevent slippage when you are scrambling up a wall. So, make sure when you go to try on a new pair of shoes that you have washed your feet, because it will be better to try them on sockless!

- Even if you have washed your feet, also realise that feet swell (Yes... SWELL... as well as SMELL). So, if you try on a pair of shoes when your feet are cold, they may fit in a size smaller than if you try on the same pair after for example, a long walk.

- If possible, stand on a hold or protruding edge. Your toes are the most important part of the foot for climbing, so make sure you can comfortably balance on them. If you're trying them on in a shop connected to a climbing gym, ask to have a practice climb in them.

- Your foot should fill the shoe. Expect to have a tighter fit than normal shoes. Ideally, you should be able to feel your toes snug, but not crushed, at the end of the shoe. For more aggressive shoes, expect your toes to be curled at the end (downwards, but definitely not upwards!).

- There should be no 'dead space' within the shoe. Feel the area around your heel and across the top of your foot: loose or baggy material is a sure sign that the shoe is too large. If you have narrow feet, try 'low volume' models.

- Press your finger lightly against the rubber bottom of your shoe, from the toes to the heel. If you cannot feel the touch of your finger, it may be an indication that there is a gap between the sole of your foot and the bottom of the shoe.

- Bear in mind that climbing shoes become less rigid and will stretch with wear: leather shoes will stretch a lot more than synthetic ones.

- **BEWARE:** Some climbers INSIST climbing shoes should be so tight they hurt! Let's be clear:

Climbing shoes may not be as comfortable as a pair of luxurious fur slippers but they shouldn't cause pain. SNUG is GOOD, PAIN is BAD. Pain could be a signal you are damaging your feet, and, if you're a youngster, it's important not to squash them into something that's going to affect normal growth. If it physically hurts to climb, you're hardly likely to climb to your full potential.

And besides, even if you do manage to crush your feet into a pair of ultra-painful, badass climbing shoes, whenever you take them off, you're going to have to deal with onlookers screaming and throwing up at the sight of your hideously deformed tootsies! It's at times like this that you will realise the benefit and importance of a good climbing shoe fitter... if you do find someone in store who has the knowledge and PATIENCE to allow you to try shoe after shoe after shoe to find THE ONE, then you will be as well to remember them for future purchases!

Finally... CLEAN YOUR SHOES!

I hark back to – not so fond – memories of my childhood, forced to polish my school shoes EVERY SINGLE DAY. So, it comes as a blessed relief that climbing shoes require relatively little attention. So, when I say, "clean your shoes" I just mean, make sure you wipe any dirt or grime off the soles before each climb. The rubber soles of climbing shoes are designed to stick to the surface you are climbing. Anything that gets in between your shoe rubber and the rock (artificial or real) – mud, grit, dust, banana skin, baloney sandwich, etc - will reduce the amount of friction between the two, basically making them less 'sticky'. They might also benefit from the odd wipe down with a damp cloth and, given that sockless, they can cause feet to sweat, 'odour eaters' may be a sound investment (anyone with working olfactory sense will be thankful).

CHALK

If you are reading this then, frankly, very well done! I mean, I can't believe I've written a whole section about chalk?! But the fact of the matter is: chalk is an essential subject for climbers.

When your hands are sweaty or greasy, they are less able to grip. Chalk helps absorb the moisture from your skin, keeping your hands dry, and therefore better able to grip onto surfaces. Now, this isn't the stuff teachers used to scrawl on a blackboard. That's made from Calcium Carbonate (CaCO3) which dissolves in water and would be absolutely rubbish for climbing (it would just dissolve on sweaty mitts!) The chalk used for rock climbing is Magnesium Carbonate (MgCO3), which doesn't dissolve, keeping your hands so dry you could climb up a wall of jelly... well, maybe not, but you'd probably get further than if you had no chalk at all.

Go onto the internet and search: "climbing chalk" and lo and behold, a dizzying array of brands that all claim to be better than the others. Seriously, it's all Magnesium Carbonate... it shouldn't be that difficult, should it?! Well, know that chalk comes in a few forms:

Chalk balls

I know... it sounds like something Great Uncle Arthur had to go to the doctor for... Actually, chalk balls are small fabric sacks in the shape of:

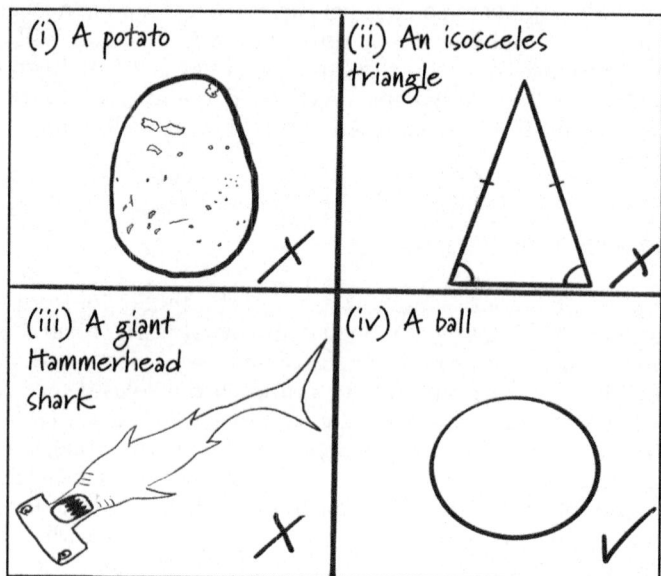

Chalk balls are filled with powdered chalk which escapes through the porous material in small amounts. The main benefit of a chalk ball is that it limits the amount of chalk dust in the air, and you won't risk spilling it all over the place, which is more than can be said for…

Powdered chalk

Powdered chalk is crushed chalk that isn't living inside a chalk ball! It's basically loose chalk – free to run wild over the Great Plains… or, ideally, in a 'chalk bag'. Powdered chalk, contained within a bespoke material chalk bag, is probably the most common means by which climbers carry their chalk. Easily transportable, climbers carry them between climbs or tie them around their waist, dipping their hands into the bag whenever required to guarantee a thorough covering.

Powdered chalk varies in texture depending on how finely the chalk has been crushed or whether it contains any additives, such as drying agents. Whilst easily accessible, beware of overfilling your chalk bag – you don't want chalk spilling out every time you dip your hands in. Or worse still, kicking over your bag (something I do regularly) and seeing it spread all over the floor. Believe me, picking up chalk is akin to trying to pick up dust!

Compressed block

Although less commonly used, the benefit of obtaining a solid, compressed block of chalk is that you can break a lump off and crush it up as fine or as chunky as you require, safe in the knowledge that the rest of the block won't blow away in a strong gust of wind.

Liquid chalk

Using liquid chalk for the first time is like becoming a member of the Magic Circle: you squirt some of the chalk goo on your hands and nothing happens… but wait for it… and suddenly, "HEY PRESTO!", you look like you have put on a pair of white gloves!

Liquid chalk contains alcohol which instantly evaporates when applied to your hands, leaving them coated with a layer of chalk. It is less messy than powdered chalk (unless you squash the bottle in your bag and it explodes all over your sandwiches), and is great for giving your hands a complete covering without leaving a cloud of dust in the air. But BEWARE: if you have any cuts on your hands, the alcohol will really make them STING!

Another key consideration in using liquid chalk with high alcohol content is that it makes for an effective hand sanitiser. Bacteria and other nasties can survive on surfaces for seconds, minutes, hours, or days depending on the environment. So, whilst you certainly shouldn't rely on liquid chalk to keep your hands clean, it's a step in the right direction, and should help give you that extra peace of mind when climbing, particularly on commonly used routes.

No chalk

Well, it's not like chalk is a requirement. We're all different – I've got horribly sweaty mitts, so I like to have some chalk readily available. But if you're lucky you may have naturally dry hands and need not fork out on any chalk at all!

Whatever you decide on, be advised, over-chalking your hands will make you LOSE FRICTION. Don't go crazy…. a fine layer is enough!

Chalk bags

I used to carry around a chalk ball, dropping it on the mat before each climb, a plume of chalk dust signalling my arrival. Any novice climber should recognise this as a social FAUX PAS (zat is French for a BLUNDER… ooo la la!). Similarly, clapping your hands to create HUGE PLUMES OF CHALK DUST may look pretty, but if everyone did it, the whole place would quickly look like a scene out of Steven King's 'The FOG' (minus the horrifically scary monsters) and potentially lead to a coughing frenzy. It's important to CONTROL YOUR CHALK. Although not so much of an issue with liquid chalk (unless you purposefully squirt it all over the place), loose chalk can be more problematic, which is why a chalk bag is a good investment.

Chalk bags come in various shapes and sizes… If you're doing short climbing routes, as in bouldering, then you may just need to add a bit of chalk at the start of the climb.

Many boulderers like to purchase a larger, standalone bag, often referred to as a BOULDER BUCKET.

For sustained climbing, such as on a high wall, climbers tend to opt for smaller and somewhat lighter chalk bags which hang off a belt around the waist.

It's a matter of personal choice but, you'll soon realise, it's better getting a bag that's PRACTICAL rather than one that's on sale, branded or just makes you laugh (although there is always something highly entertaining about placing your hand into the 'mouth' of a googly eyed monster chalk bag).

Consider:

- A bag with pockets may be useful to hold other useful items, like finger tape or valuables such as your wallet, phone, keys, or lucky rabbit's foot.

- A bag with a 'brush loop' allows you to store… a brush… to clean holds, not your teeth (unless you have extremely high dental hygiene standards). Holds can become dirty and/or sweaty so having 'boulder brush' allows you rub the surface for much needed friction. Bear in mind that if you were planning to wear the chalk bag, in the event of a fall, a brush could be an unnecessary hazard.

- A bag with a cord and toggle allows you to close it when not in use, thereby stopping the escape of thousands of tonnes of climbing chalk over the period of your lifetime…

"Climbing shoes?"

"CHECK!"

"Chalk?"

"CHECK!"

"Then it's time to start climbing?!!!"

The least you need to know

- If you've just begun climbing, it may be more cost effective to hire climbing shoes, although purchasing a pair will help ensure you get ones that fit better.

- The better the fit, the better you are likely to be able to climb, so it's important to 'try before you buy'.

- There are three types of climbing shoe: neutral, aggressive, and moderate.

- A climber uses chalk on their hands to draw moisture from the skin and thereby promote better friction on the (artificial or real) rock.

- Chalk comes in various forms including in a porous ball, loose powder, solid block, or liquid form.

3

UNDER COVER CLIMBER: CLIMBING IN A ROCK GYM

Indoor climbing gyms are a great introductory route into climbing. This chapter will help you understand:

- What to wear... and what not to wear.
- Hazards of an indoor climbing environment.
- Essential features of a climbing gym, including the grade system.
- The importance of warming up and warming down.
- How to fall safely (yes... I did say fall)!

So, you've made it to the climbing gym and you take a look around....there are a few Tarzan-types confidently bounding up the walls, cool dudes huddled in a group fist bumping every third person whilst loudly describing their most gnarly climbs, and an old guy/gal so ancient that they'd look better suited in the Egyptian Mummy section of the local museum... and yet they're climbing as well as the next person.

When you're just starting out, it's easy to feel a bit SELF-CONSCIOUS. I didn't start climbing until I was 40, whereas my youngest daughter was only 7. Just remember - everyone has to start somewhere. Just being there is a giant step. I recall my first climbing experience being overwhelming. It was challenging enough just clinging on to the holds let alone listening to instructions and 'advice' given by friends and onlookers. So cut yourself some slack and concentrate on grasping the basics, because these will provide the foundation for the FUTURE YOU...

Also, you need to realise straight away that, whilst everyone at the climbing gym might LOOK like they know what they are doing, there's a fair chance a lot of them will be using bad technique, climbing outside their comfort zone, or are a few moves short of hurting themselves! You, however, (a) have already demonstrated the FORESIGHT of a DEMIGOD having invested in this marvellous book and (b) will no doubt, put into action the old Chinese proverb, "He who asks a question is a fool for 5 minutes; he who does not ask a question remains a fool forever." Climbing gyms have dedicated and experienced staff, many of whom will be nuts about climbing, and pleased to be asked any question, however daft you might think it sounds.

If you know someone with experience of climbing, then it may help to have them tag along to give you the benefit of their own knowledge. Although, when I say, "experience of climbing", ideally, whoever you choose to go with will have had some professional instruction, or else they could teach bad habits, become a hindrance, or worse still, be a hazard in their own right!

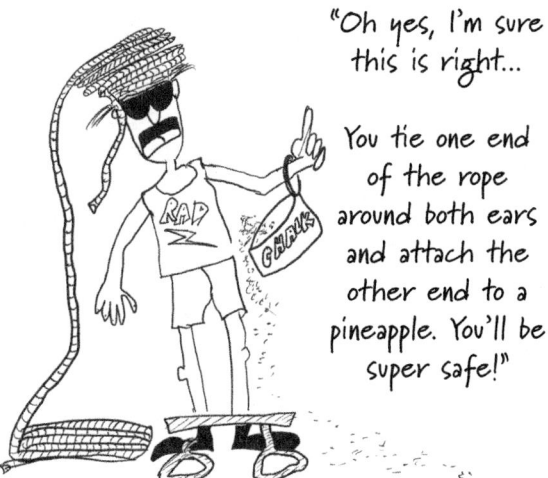

Do I look the part?

Clothing choice is only important to the extent that you don't want to wear anything impractical. So, it may be your favourite 3-metre pashmina, but if there's a chance it's going to get caught on a hold and garrotte you, probably best leave it at home.

A poor choice in climbing clothing

Similarly, even if you do look fabulous in your ultratight skinny jeans, chances are they will impede normal leg movement, so give them a miss as well!

You could easily go crazy and spend A LOT of money on designer brand bespoke 'climber' clothes, but loose and/or light fitting clothing like a t-shirt and cotton jogging bottoms are a good start. The temperature of a climbing gym is likely to be regulated, so you can be assured you don't need to dress for the arctic.

BLING, BLING... BLING, BLING...

Remove all jewellery before you go climbing. The problem with climbing wearing rings, bracelets, bangles, or watches is that they can snag or get caught on a hold. Doesn't sound too awful, does it?

"OOOooooooo, I snagged my wedding ring..."

Well, DEGLOVING is a very real, hideously unpleasant injury that can result when a climber catches their ring on a hold. If a ring gets stuck and a climber falls, then it can have a nasty habit of cutting the flesh clean off the bone of the finger... Cue BARF! Fancy scooping up the soft, fleshy remains of your finger and trying to squash it back on to the bone of your pinkie? No? Then don't wear a ring or any other jewellery that could get caught!

Once you've taken off your jewellery, put it somewhere safe, but don't climb with anything in your pockets – keys, coins, glasses, framed picture of your sweetheart - if you fall, you're going to land on them. Okay, and for the smartass who says, "I'm going to climb with an inflatable mattress in my pocket", get to the back of the class!

Choose a safe path

Indoor climbing gyms are attractive because they offer a rich variety of climbs, for different levels of ability, in a relatively confined area. The only issue with this is that they can get very busy at peak times (generally 1700-2100 hours weekdays and all-day weekends). Consequently, it pays to be aware of your surroundings and other climbers. If there is a designated path to get to a climb (e.g. an obvious walkway or different coloured flooring): USE IT. That's right folks… it's not there for looks.

Climbing areas are often marked or taped off, so stay out of the 'climbing zone' until you are actually ready to climb (e.g. after you have removed your 3-metre pashmina, 12-inch hoop earrings, assortment of chunky gold rings and ultratight jeans). And even when you are in the climbing zone, it's good practice to stay a little back from the wall… other than when you are climbing.

Never walk or stand directly below a climber… doesn't matter how good they are… it's still going to hurt if they fall and land on your HEAD!

In climbing gyms with rope climbing areas (the use of ropes being the main give away here), generally keep away from the belayers (i.e. the individuals holding the rope… ergo… keeping the climber safe) so that you don't distract them whilst they are (SHOULD BE!) concentrating on the climber.

"I had enough trouble just crossing the road to get here!"

- 28 -

In bouldering climbing areas there are no ropes or belayers to alert you to the presence of a climber, so be particularly wary of people jumping or falling off the walls. They will be relying on the fact that the ground is clear beneath them, so periodically LOOK UP... to check that the path ahead of you is safe... and DOWN AGAIN to avoid tripping over chalk bags, mats, and people!

You're getting waaaaaarmmmmmm.... (Warm-ups!)

Do you get out of bed in the morning and instantly run 2 miles down the road, or watch TV for an hour and then, in the blink of an eye, jump in your pool and swim 1000 metres?

If the answer is "yes", then (a) you're a better man/woman/child/lifeform than me and (b) WOW! You have a TV and a SWIMMING POOL... lucky!!! (Although, having a TV by your swimming pool is extremely dangerous didn't you know?). If the answer is "no" (which, frankly, is what I am looking for here), then I'm glad, because you really should do a WARM-UP before any vigorous activity – running, swimming, football, hockey, dancing, athletics, robbing a bank, tennis, and CLIMBING.

To avoid injury and prepare your body for climbing activity you need to raise your heart rate and body temperature. Watching a horror movie with the heating on doesn't count. You're going to be putting your body under different stresses and strains to normal (unless you happen to have been raised by apes) and a warm-up will help reduce the risk of injury to your muscles, tendons, and joints.

Getting your body temperature up doesn't have to be arduous or boring - a game of Frisbee (outside... and it's more fun when you're not on your own!), catching a ball or even jogging on the spot can be quite sufficient. I like skipping... not hand in hand to the musical 'The Sound of Music'... I mean skipping on the spot with a nylon cord. It's a favourite warm up for boxers. Whilst there is little need to be punching anyone in the head during your climbing session (hopefully), skipping is a good way of quickly getting the heart beating and warms up the shoulder joints (key usage in climbing). You can just use the end of an old climbing rope and jump over that. Just be careful no one is on the other end of it! Whatever you choose, you don't need to go CRAZY... we're not talking about BEASTING yourself to the point of exhaustion! It's simply a PULSE RAISER. It's after the pulse raiser that you'll be beasting yourself... Nah, only joking!

Let me be honest with you... I HATE WARM-UPS. As soon as I see the climbing wall / rock face I'm super excited to just get on and climb. H-o-w-e-v-e-r... after I sprained my finger, elbow, shoulder, ankle, knee, wrist, etc, I finally cottoned on to the fact that they are a NECESSARY EVIL. And, quite simply, you will climb better after a proper warm-up. So, I have prepared a very simple step-by-step warm up below. I guarantee my warm-up guide is NOT going to take HOURS or DESTROY YOU! Yes, there are a BILLION other different exercises you could do, but this is a good starter for ten. You can supplement the exercises outlined for ones that you prefer, so long as your 'exercise' involves targeting those parts of the body that are key to climbing, namely the fingers and hands, arms and shoulders, hips, and legs. Climbing can be tough on the muscles, tendons, and joints, so stimulating them into readiness will help them cope and prevent the likelihood of injury.

Warm-up exercises

1. Star jumps (20 times)

Imagine you are popping out of a cake or taking part in an 80's dance video if it helps, but these dynamic movements will get the muscles working, major joints loosened, and your heartbeat turned up a notch.

Simply stand with your legs shoulder width apart and your arms by your side. Then JUMP your feet outwards at the same time as you raise your arms to form a STAR (ahhhh... beautiful!)

2. Spotty dogs (20 times)

Yeah, I literally have no idea why they're called 'Spotty dogs' (at least a star jump is vaguely star-like), but they are a similarly great exercise to kick start your body into action.

With your right foot forward and right arm raised in the air, jump and switch positions, so that your left leg is forward and your left arm is raised. Repeat, repeatedly!

3. Roll your arms forward (10 times)

This should be a smooth controlled motion – you are aiming to mobilise the shoulder joint for action - you aren't trying to take off, although granted, that would be impressive.

4. Roll your arms backwards (10 times)

Yep... the other way. Simple, heh?!

**5. Roll arms in opposite directions
(10 times each way)**

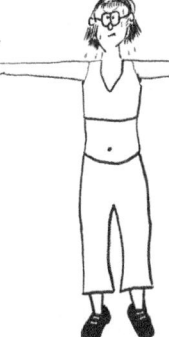

**6. Wrist rolls
(10 times each way)**

This may completely flummox you at first, but once mastered, you can amaze and impress onlookers with your advanced Chinook helicopter action.

Roll your right arm forwards and left arm backwards 10 times, and then, reverse the action. Is there no end to your arm rolling talent?

Reach your arms out to the sides so that your shoulders are level. Rotate your wrists in a circular motion clockwise and then anti-clockwise.

**7. Finger clenches
(3 x 10 times)**

Clench your fists and extend your fingers repeatedly, with your arms:

(i) by your side (10 times).
(ii) raised to 90-degrees (10 times).
(iii) above your head (10 times).

You should really feel the PUMP in your forearms as you work your finger flexors (fists) and extensors (high-fives), whist at the same time looking like a crazed bidder at an auction.

8. Hip roll (10 times each direction)

Twirl an imaginary Hoola-hoop and rotate your hips in a circular motion clockwise and then anti-clockwise.

9. Bear walk (1 minute)

Lean forward, placing your hands on the floor so that your weight is distributed between your arms and your legs. Keeping your legs and arms straight (your arms are now officially legs for the purpose of this exercise) and your hips high, 'walk' slowly forwards, backwards, and sideways. The bear walk is good for shoulder and wrist mobility. If you feel self-conscious, pretend you're looking for a dropped coin or earring. If you're not self-conscious, then intermittently stand on your haunches and 'roar' at passers-by.

10. Reverse lunge (10 each leg)

So, imagine you're about to get knighted by the King for your 'outstanding contribution to rock climbing'. Keeping your back straight, take a wide step back with one leg and drop your knee so that it hovers a couple of inches off the ground. At the same time lower your front knee into a 90-degree angle. Hold the position briefly before coming back into a standing position, moving your back foot next to your lead foot. You can either repeat on the same leg or swap legs. Hold your hands out in front of you or rest them on your hips during this exercise (Alternatively, wave them all over the place as you wobble uncontrollably with each lunge). This is a really good way of waking up your legs and core, which will be essential in driving your body up the wall when you start climbing.

11. Front leg swing (10 each leg)

Hold on to a wall or something to steady your balance (a willing friend will do) and, keeping your leg straight, swing it forwards and backwards. Make sure the leg you are standing on is also kept straight, with your foot flat on the floor. This will help mobilise your hips and legs as well as putting you in good stead for a job as a Moulin Rouge Can-Can dancer. Make sure you have plenty of room to execute the move so as to avoid booting any passers-by in the head!

12. Side leg swing (10 each leg)

Keeping your leg straight, swing it from side to side. This is a dynamic stretch which will also help loosen your hip joint, but ensure you swing your leg to the point you feel a stretch and no further. Your legs don't often move in these directions so best to have a measured approach.

Finished? You can either begin climbing on easy routes or REPEAT the above until you feel sufficiently warmed up.

Warm-up Part deux

Once you've done your warm-up, then you need to warm-up again… this time 'on the rocks'. Basically, don't think because your heart's beating faster and you're a little out of breath, that you're ready to ascend the hardest climbing problems in sight. You need to build up the difficulty level slowly. This way you give those specific muscles, joints, and tendons required for climbing time to acclimatise. Whilst I've no doubt you could just jump straight on the hardest route, the simple fact is, your body will appreciate a gradual increase in difficulty….

"I've done 10 star jumps and 10 leg swings... let's smash this climb!"

Starting on easier routes also gives your MIND time to prepare. Climbing requires focus. You don't want to be halfway up a NAILS route whilst thinking about the last episode of your favourite soap, whether you left the oven on, or where you left your skinny jeans. You want your mind and body to work in perfect synchrony, so it makes sense to move steadily from basic to harder routes. This will help your mind relax and begin to focus on the important tasks at hand: balance, movement, and coordination. And if you're still not convinced, then consider the very climbing specific sensation of getting 'PUMPED'.

Doesn't sound particularly pleasant... but I defy anyone NOT to experience the feeling at one point or another. It's a sensation you will get in your forearms, during a climb, when you reach a point where you can barely grip a pencil, let alone the next hold! It's suspected to be caused by the accumulation of lactic acid and comes a lot quicker if you haven't warmed up properly. Being pumped is an apt description because your arms will feel like they've been inflated to bursting point. But, unlike a bike tyre, sticking a nail in your arm isn't going to make any difference to the pressure. Some of the simplest ways of reducing pump include:

- Simply resting – just take a few minutes out to allow your muscles to recover.
- Doing lighter exercises, such as climbing a much easier route.
- Shaking your arms: raising them in the air and then dangling by your sides (so that gravity helps fresh blood get to the muscles).
- WARMING UP PROPERLY!

Once you've combined a warm-up with a set of easy climbs... then, and only then, "It's SHOWTIME!"

Time to START CLIMBING:

Upper grade, Retrograde, Climbing grade...

The arrangement of holds on a wall is called the route. Generally, when an individual says they're "going climbing" they mean they are going to seek out a designated route to climb. Whilst you can quite happily climb up, down, and around a climbing wall to your heart's content if you so wish, having a set start, middle, and end makes for a more focused and rewarding experience! Climbers often refer to the different routes on a wall as 'problems'. The solution to the problem is found when you unlock the right sequence of moves to get you to the top.

Every climbing route will be graded in difficulty. Grading a route is a subjective process. There isn't an independent verifier scoping the globe, comparing grades of one problem to the next, so there may be slight variations in difficulty between routes you find in one climbing gym compared to another. That's because indoor routes have been artificially created by a ROUTE SETTER, a person (or persons) who essentially think up a problem, and then attaches different shaped climbing holds onto the wall in a way designed to test the climber's ability to scale it.

A route setter can make a route easier by, for example, using larger hand and foot holds that are evenly spaced, or more difficult, by applying more testing positions or types of hold. The benefit of having a scale of difficulty is that you can map your own progress and attempt climbs that are within your capability. A climber will quickly learn to READ what is likely to be difficult just by looking at the holds, although it might not always be as obvious as you first think. I've confidently dived onto a route that I thought looked easy only to be totally flummoxed by the first hold!

"I'm guessing this one's going to be difficult..."

Fortunately, you won't have to rely on your inner DIFFICULTY-O-METER (the seventh sense?) as climbing gyms provide a visually simple guide to difficulty, usually by individually grading them or using different coloured holds, or 'tags' by the holds, to denote difficulty level (e.g. yellow for easy, green for super difficult).

It gets a little bit more scientific than that though. All climbing route grades are based on grading systems that originated from outdoor climbing, before indoor climbing gyms became popular, and none of them are based on the colour of the rock! There are multiple climbing grading systems that have been developed all over the world for different styles of climbing based on factors such as the overall difficulty of the climb, the technical climbing difficulty of the hardest move, and strenuousness (yes, that is a word). To avoid total and utter confusion I am only going to describe a couple of the most widely used grading systems for bouldering (i.e. non-rope climbing) and rope climbing (More explanation is given for the latter in Chapter 9 - I'll show you the ropes. Also, see the appendices for useful conversion charts of the most commonly used bouldering and sport climbing grade systems in Europe and the USA).

Bouldering routes are often graded on a straightforward V-SCALE, named after John 'Vermin' Sherman, and used to convey the overall difficulty of a problem, ranging from VB (VERY BASIC) to V17 (aka RIDICULOUSLY DIFFICULT). At first glance you might think to yourself, an average climber is going to climb somewhere in the middle – say, V8 or V9. WRONG! The range is more likely to be:

VB, V0, V1	Beginners...
V2, V3, V4, V5	Intermediate, including the majority of climbers on the planet...
V6, V7, V8, V9, V10	Expert, dedicated climbers...
V11, V12, V13, V14, V15	Professional climbers, lizards, monkeys, and spiders...
V16, V17	Superhumans and bizarre alien lifeforms...

Recognising the limitations at the upper end of the scale, climbing gyms (THANKFULLY) tend to set routes that reflect what most climbers would find challenging, yet still fun. No one wants to get downhearted attempting climbs that only elite athletes would ever have a chance in achieving! You should find plenty of climbs ranging from VB to V8. You want to choose a route that is – BE HONEST - in your range of ability. It's also great to try and push yourself by attempting harder routes now and then, but not to the extent that you become demotivated if they are out of your (current) level of ability.

I emphasise the fact that the route setting grades are SUBJECTIVE... a route tagged V2 is basically just what someone thinks is a V2. And as we are all different in height, weight, strength, technique, determination, coordination, tiredness on the day, hydration, to name but a few factors, it's natural that sometimes you will find a route seems hard, whilst everyone else finds it easy; and vice versa.

Many climbers find that their progress at the start of their climbing journey is exponential. They might move quickly from VB and V0 onto V1, V2, and then maybe even V3, and then suddenly they PLATEAU. The reason is simple. Determination can only take you so far. To become a GREAT climber, you need to develop understanding and practical application of technique, the right mindset, and areas of specific strength, most notably in the fingers, that can take weeks, months, and YEARS of practice to achieve. Lucky for you, you have this book to identify those foundation qualities, and the only other ingredient you really need to add is motivation.

What goes up...

Wherever possible, CLIMB DOWN, don't jump down. You'll see it, I guarantee: people scrambling to the top of a boulder problem and then just letting go... 99 times out of 100 they happily land on their feet and wander off to climb something else. Occasionally though, they land:

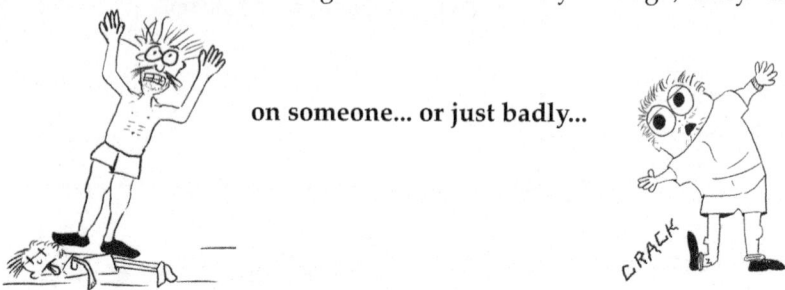

on someone... or just badly...

But don't just view climbing down from a problem as just 'being safe'. It's beneficial because you are simultaneously learning to climb in a different direction (i.e. down!) and increasing your ability to endure fatigue (reaching the top means you are only halfway through your climb).

DOWN-CLIMBING can be as tough as UP-CLIMBING. For starters, you must LEAD WITH YOUR FEET and, unless you've got a pair of eyes in your butt, it's quite difficult to see and judge foot placements on holds beneath you. However, this will really help you develop your footwork skills, which are KEY to becoming a great climber.

By the way, if you HAVE got eyes in your butt, that is super impressive – I recognise and value diversity (although the sights you must see when going to the toilet – ooooo, it doesn't bear thinking about)!

Fall out

There is one thing that everyone, to a greater or lesser extent, will worry about at some point in their climbing career, and that is FALLING. It's only natural. When climbing, you are off the ground – that beautiful stable and safe place that you normally dwell - and anything different to the NORM can result in a feeling of unease. A little bit of nervousness or anxiety about going climbing can help focus the mind, add excitement to your life, and on successful completion, an enhanced sense of achievement. However, if you get overly worried, something that should be fun can suddenly turn into something that just feels unpleasant. If you dwell on this worry too often it may adversely impact your development as a climber and may even stop you climbing altogether.

So, REALISE: worry, anxiety, and even nasty, butterfly-inducing, squeaky bottom fear is completely and utterly normal. They are instinctual reactions, designed to help you recognise and deal with danger. If you had NO FEAR, chances are you'd quite happily do all manner of daft things without truly realising the consequences, like bareback riding a crocodile, playing leapfrog in a minefield, or using your underpants as a breeding ground for tarantulas.

Once you've realised that your emotions are natural, then the second thing that you're going to need to swallow is the fact that YOU'RE GOING TO FALL. As bizarre as it might sound, for a dedicated climber, falling off becomes part of the course... if you are really going to push yourself to the limits of your climbing ability, then you're going to climb harder and harder routes, and you're going to fall off. Falling is inevitable. Obviously, you're going to do your best not to, because falling is scary – right? Well, as it happens, it doesn't have to be. If you recognise that you will fall, you can prepare yourself to fall and land correctly and safely. This confidence will make the possibility and the act of falling a lot easier.

Falling whilst bouldering, is different to falling whilst rope climbing; the main point being you're always going to land on the ground as you don't have a rope to stop you. Therefore, where you are going to land if you do fall off, is a very important question. Climbing over bamboo spikes, broken glass, or a pit of vipers is ill-advised, whereas climbing over the soft matting in a climbing gym or the equivalent 'boulder mat' outdoors, is going to dramatically reduce any chance of injury.

How to fall whilst rock climbing*

*Bet this book wouldn't sell if it had that title!

Once you realise you're falling, ACCEPT YOUR FATE:

- **DON'T** be fooled by the apparent success of hunky movie action heroes leaping from a helicopter/tall building/train onto a window ledge/bridge/passing vehicle... if you try and grab other holds on your way down, you're likely to wrench your fingers, arms, or shoulders.

- **DON'T** tense up - As spectacular as you might look in a tight-fitting leotard with your hair in a bun, you are NOT landing a GYMNASTIC POSE; you don't want to be rigid.

- **DON'T** be tempted to put your arm out to save yourself. Granted, it is a natural reaction, particularly if you are falling sideways. But you are much more likely to sprain or even break a limb in this way. Remember, you are falling onto soft matting specifically designed for falls.

- **DO** try and land squarely on both feet, ideally at least shoulder width apart – there is less chance of rolling on an ankle if both legs are engaged.

- **DO** keep your arms tucked into your chest.

- **DO** bend your knees slightly – these amazing lower limbs come to the rescue as great big shock absorbers.

- **DO** roll – backwards, sideways, or even forwards – the roll itself will help dissipate the energy generated from your body into the floor.

- And finally – though it may sound like the hardest thing of all...

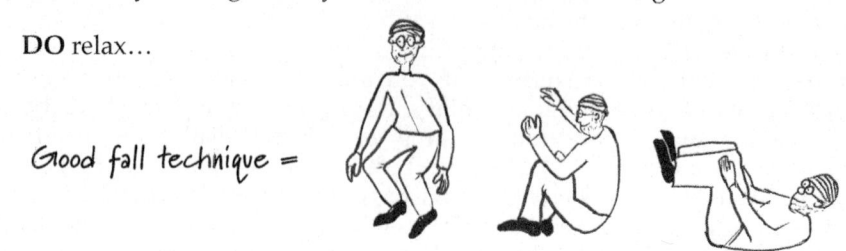

    DO relax...

Good fall technique =

Ironically, if you're thinking about falling, you're not giving your full attention to your actual climbing, making it MORE LIKELY that you will fall! So, it can be useful to practice falling, to help put your mind at rest and realise that it's not as bad as you might think.

I'm not talking here about swan diving off the top of the highest point in the climbing gym by the way. But, I would encourage 'dropping off', in a controlled manner, at a point where it feels safe and comfortable to do so. Obviously ensure you clear the ground beneath you - that includes kit and people - and then 'fall' off the wall at progressively higher stages.

Bad fall technique =

Spot the spotter

Having a SPOTTER can also impact positively on your safety. SPOTTING is the term given to someone tasked with the specific role of helping a falling climber to land safely. A fall can be quite sudden and unexpected, so looking for a good landing place whilst sailing through the air is a big ask, particularly when you're probably still wondering what happened. A good spotter is someone who remains close by the climber, watching them intently as they progress up a route, and reacts instantly when they fall. Don't worry, it doesn't mean that as a spotter you must physically catch the climber. And you should, as a matter of principal, also strenuously avoid the climber landing on you!

Communication is key… a spotter may be poised and ready, but if a climber thinks they're going to fall, they should say so – a bit of notice goes a long way!

To spot:

Get into a boxer's stance: Place one foot in front of the other with your knees bent, and raise your hands, although no need to wear gloves.

Keep your arms slightly bent. Bent legs and arms will better cope with absorbing any impact of the falling climber. The aim is to get a firm grasp on the climber's shoulders, midriff, hips, stomach, underneath the arms, or even the butt will do if it helps you guide them to the ground… although, be advised, repeated 'butt catches' could give you a bad name!

You want to try and keep the falling climber upright, protecting against any chance of head, neck, or spinal injury, so grabbing someone's legs is ill-advised as you might cause the climber to flip over and land face first. Catching someone by the neck or head is equally, if not more dangerous, and unlikely to generate positive reviews!

Just one final thing to remember if you're spotting… SPOT! It isn't a wildly exciting role, but if you've said you'll do it, you need to be laser-locked on from the moment the climber starts until the moment they finish.

At the end of the day (it gets dark... and you need to warm-down)

Soooooo, you could end your session on a route so hard that your fingernails rip off, you burst a blood vessel in your eye lurching for the final move, and your knees buckle in two when you half fall, half jump down at the end. Climbing whilst fatigued is a surefire way of picking up an injury. A much better idea is to conclude your session with some easy climbs followed by some light stretching. A gradual reduction in exertion should help your body relax, and stretching not only promotes recovery but helps prevent tight muscles and inflexibility, two things you want to avoid if you want to excel at climbing.

I have a memory like a goldfish... uhhhhh...

I have a memory like a goldfish, so when stretching different parts of my body after a climbing session, I'd often forget about doing my shoulders one day and then remember the next time, but instead forget to stretch my calves. I was coming away with a semi-stretched body (although better than no stretching I guess). Nowadays I follow a set routine, stretching in sequence from my head to my toes so I am less likely to miss an area. Chapter 13, under subtitle 'Flexibility', provides a stretching routine that targets all the areas that are likely to get tense through climbing.

P.S. Before you start stretching, take off your climbing shoes. A tight pair of climbing shoes won't help you relax... and make sure you leave them a short distance away - you don't want the stench of sweaty feet putting you off either!

The least you need to know

- Remember: everyone must start somewhere. Take your time and nail the basics.

- Wear suitable light or loose-fitting clothing and ditch all jewellery.

- Warm-up: you will climb better for it.

- Bouldering routes are graded for difficulty on the V scale.

- Falling is a natural part of the process. Accept this, practice, and it will become second nature.

- Warm-down and stretch: your body will thank you for it.

4

HOLD ON... WHAT? CLIMBING WALL FEATURES

Whether you climb up the features of a rock face or the artificial holds of an indoor climbing gym, there are certain wall angles and hold shapes that will be instantly recognisable. So much so, that they have individual names, and it's as well to get to know them. It can sometimes feel like another language, but the more you climb, the better you will be at recognising these common features, and ultimately able to determine the best techniques to climb them. This chapter will give you an understanding of:

- The different types of wall angle.
- The names and shapes of common holds.
- The best way to use each hold type.
- A technique for when there are no holds (palming).

What's your angle?

There are 3 basic variations in the angle of a wall or rock face that a climber will encounter, and you won't need a protractor to work out which one is which:

Vertical wall

A straight up, 90-degree vertical wall is probably the first thing that comes to mind when anyone talks about climbing.

"Climbed my first slab!"

Slab

Anything LESS THAN 90-degrees, is technically a slab, but given the difference between 1 – 89 degrees, the slope of the slab can vary dramatically!

Overhang

With varying degrees of steepness, overhangs are where the wall slopes out towards you, at an angle more than 90 degrees. Overhangs can be so 'overhangy' that you're climbing parallel to the floor. This is sometimes referred to as climbing "on the roof", although climbing "on the ceiling" would be more appropriate.

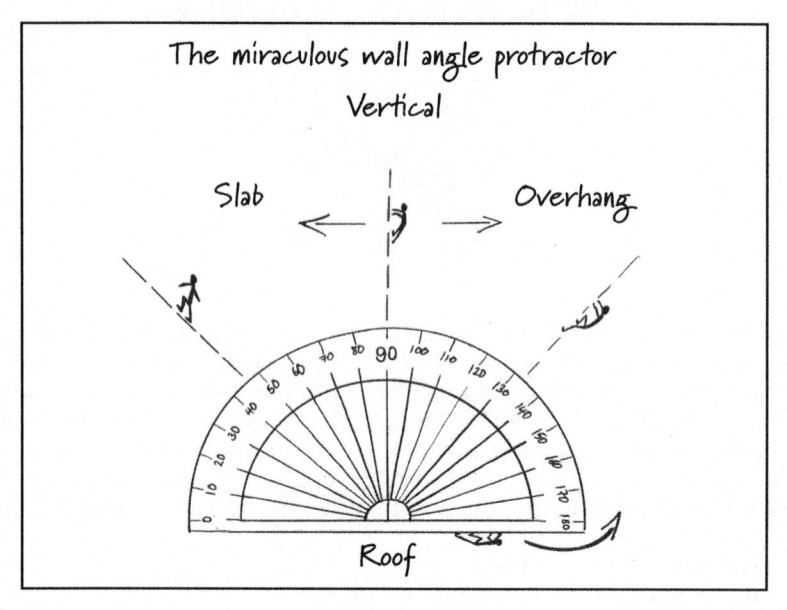

The miraculous wall angle protractor

Vertical

Slab ← → Overhang

Roof

Many climbing gyms will include a CAVE, an interesting but physically demanding route, where you ascend a wall, cross the roof, and then come out of the mouth of the cave.

Although it's basic stuff, just knowing the key differences in wall angles is useful because, not only does the technique applied to climbing each type of wall vary, they are often used as points of reference. So now at least you SHOULD know if someone says, "Meet you by the overhang?" you'll go to the correct area...

NOT the correct 'overhang' meeting point!

Outdoor climbing involves going to a cliff or boulder and climbing on a rock face that is largely unchangeable, save for occasional alterations caused by, for example, natural erosion. Climbers travel to different locations to experience a diversity of climbs.

Indoor climbing gyms offer the opportunity to climb at the same location on an artificial rock face that can be altered to provide different climbing experiences. Each climbing gym has its own unique wall layout. Often the selling point will be high walls, a large bouldering area, or specialised features, like a huge overhang. Most climbing gym walls are comprised of a wooden or fibreglass surface upon which climbing holds are screwed or bolted. Some go one step further and have 'feature walls' which and are made to look like a real cliff or boulder, complete with indentations, grooves, cracks, and hollows that you might see on real rock.

Wall layout does not tend to change much because that would require costly alterations to what are, in effect, safety tested permanent structures. However, the way holds appear on the wall can be changed. An indoor climbing gym can completely change the climbs on their walls by detaching and reattaching holds in different arrangements, thereby providing a limitless diversity of climbing experiences.

Types of hold

A variety of commonly shaped holds can be found at both indoor and outdoor climbing venues. It is useful to get to know them because it will help you identify the difficulty of a route and how best to climb it:

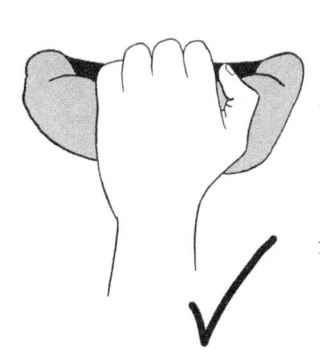

Jug

A jug is a deep handhold which is generally easy to hold on to. Jugs are a climber's best friend because they are reassuringly good to grip or step on.

Sloper

The sloper is the EVIL NEMESIS of the jug! Slopers are rounded holds with no obvious edge of any kind, making them a unique and often frustrating challenge. Slopers are best climbed with an open hand grip to get as much surface area in contact with the hold. Make use of any nodules or dimples in the hold, however tiny, because it may just be enough to help you hold on. If you can involve your thumb to pinch the hold this will also assist.

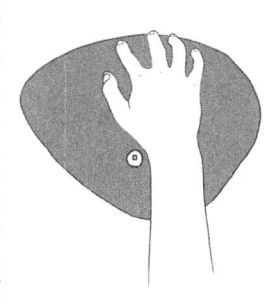

Crimp

A crimp is a small edge. Like any hold, they can vary in size, but generally you will only be able to get one or two pads of your fingers on them... if you're lucky! Crimps can place immense pressure on the finger joints and tendons so ensure your fingers are properly warmed up before using them.

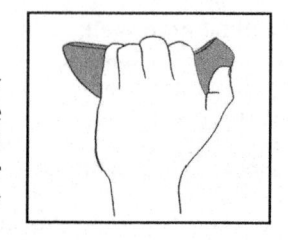

Side pull

Take a wild guess! Whilst most holds might rely on downwards pressure, the trick to getting the most out of a side pull is pulling in an opposite direction to the hold.... pulling down isn't going to work... pulling sideways will.

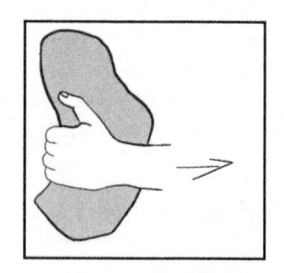

Gaston

I always think a 'gaston' sounds more like something that should be in the engine of a car. A gaston is the opposite of a side pull... in fact, rather, it's a side push. To be clear – climbing hold or engine part – all you really need to know is that you should push your body away from this side hold rather than pull yourself towards it.

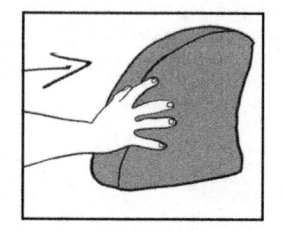

Imagine if you will, a circus strongman gets trapped in a lift...

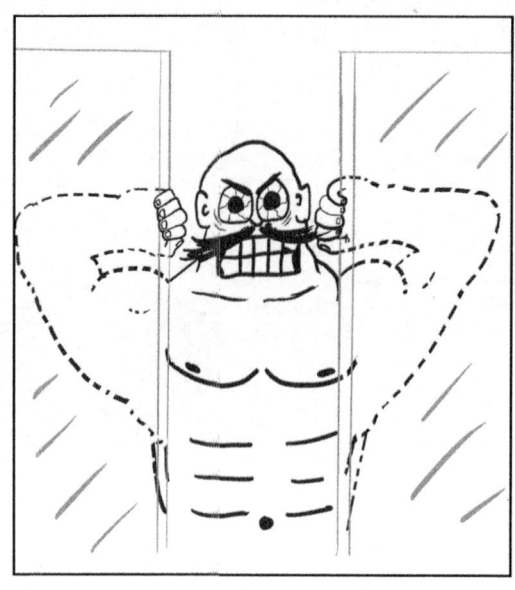

Whilst he might consider pummelling a hole in the steel doors, it doesn't sit well with his tough, but family friendly image.

Appreciating he could just press the emergency buzzer for assistance, he might also try prising open the doors, ably demonstrating the position required for a double gaston.

"Thanks strongman...

Next time, use the stairs!"

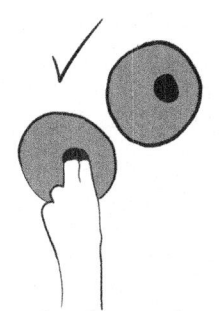

Pocket

A hold with a hole in it! You can fit a finger, hand, or foot in it depending on the size of the hole relative to the size of your finger, hand, or foot. It could even be big enough to fit your head in but that is not recommended!

Smaller pockets may only provide enough space for one or two fingers... at a squeeze! So, be EXTRA CAREFUL if you're new to climbing, or already tired and worn from a session on the rocks - the pressure on the tendons and ligaments of those tiny digits can be immense - and a likely path to injury if your body isn't ready for the challenge.

Pinch

A pinch is a hold that is gripped by squeezing your fingers and thumb on opposite sides.

Undercut

An undercut, also known as an undercling, is like an upside down hold... a hold you grip from underneath (i.e. the palm of your hand will be facing up rather than down). It's precisely because the hold is upside down that you pull up on the hold rather than pulling down.

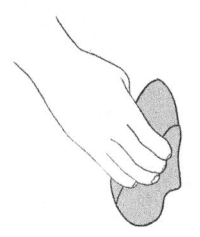

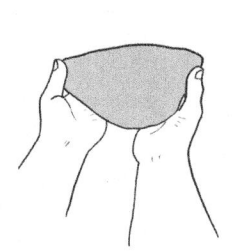

Since you're pulling up in a bid to defy gravity, it's important to get your feet high and push hard against the wall, maintaining a rigid body tension as you reach for the next hold.

Uppercut

A powerful punch on the chin - definitely NOT a hold, and best avoided when climbing! Only included because I guarantee that after reading this at some point you will call an *undercut* an *uppercut* and then it won't just be me who does it!

- 45 -

Volumes

Volumes are three-dimensional features attached to a climbing wall upon which other holds can be affixed, and can be used as holds in their own right. They widely vary in size and shape and can therefore radically change the shape of the wall. For example, prism shaped volumes are a common sight and can be used to change a section of vertical wall into a slab climb.

If there is a volume on a wall, general rule of thumb is that you can use it as if it were part of the existing wall. You can use all sides of the volume, but it often requires additional thought and planning because the direction of pull/push isn't always immediately obvious.

You won't find any volumes outdoors. They are an indoor climbing phenomenon, which speaks volumes of how far the sport has come (That was bad, even for me).

Footholds

Whilst you can invariably stand on any hand hold to assist your ascent, there will also be holds that are specifically for your feet. These tend to be much smaller in comparison. It's not uncommon to hear people complaining that a handhold is "rubbish". Often, they've just read the route incorrectly and are wrongly attempting to use a foothold with their hands. A basic, but reliable rule of thumb is: if you can't hold it with your hands, it's probably a foot hold… but bear in mind it might just be a difficult-to-hold-handhold!

Holding a hold…

I assure you… this is not a 'teaching your grandmother to suck eggs' moment! I know you know how to *hold* a hold… with your hands… right?!

There are still a few useful points to consider while you're doing the holding, including: (i) the amount of pressure used, (ii) using your fingers and thumbs, (iii) the direction of pull, (iv) the position of your arms, and (v) how to move when there are no holds at all.

(i)   **Under pressure**

The first thing to be conscious of is exactly how tightly you are gripping each hold. When I feel under pressure or nervous climbing a new route, I have a bad habit of squeezing so tight it's a wonder either the hold or my hands don't EXPLODE under the pressure. Quite aside from the mess an exploding hand or hold would create, the harder you squeeze, the more your muscles tense, and the quicker you will tire yourself out. Conversely, if you don't hold tight enough, you're going to fall straight off the wall, so it's important to get the right balance!

Applying the right pressure is something that you can only achieve with practice, so make a conscious effort to concentrate on your grip, using only enough pressure than is necessary to keep you in place. If you're climbing a slab, you may barely need to squeeze at all, whereas an overhang is going to need much more pressure. Figure out what is going to be most efficient in any given circumstance.

(ii) **All fingers and thumbs**

The more you climb, the stronger your fingers will get, but because your little finger tends to be comparatively smaller and weaker than the rest, some climbers don't use it at all. Okay, so your pinkie isn't going to singularly hold you on the wall, and frankly it's not great for nose picking or poking people in the eye, but it would be daft not to harness its collective power! LOVE AND USE YOUR PINKIE! Similarly, don't forget your thumb! The power that this opposing digit provides shouldn't be underestimated. You won't fair well on a pinch hold if you disregard one half of the pinch!

(iii) **One Direction**

Give some thought to the direction you pull on a hold. It's easy to think that you would always pull down as you propel yourself upwards, in the same way you might on the rungs of a ladder, but this isn't always the case. You want to be creating the maximum OPPOSING FORCES against the hold so, if it is a left-facing diagonal crimp, you want to be pulling diagonally right.

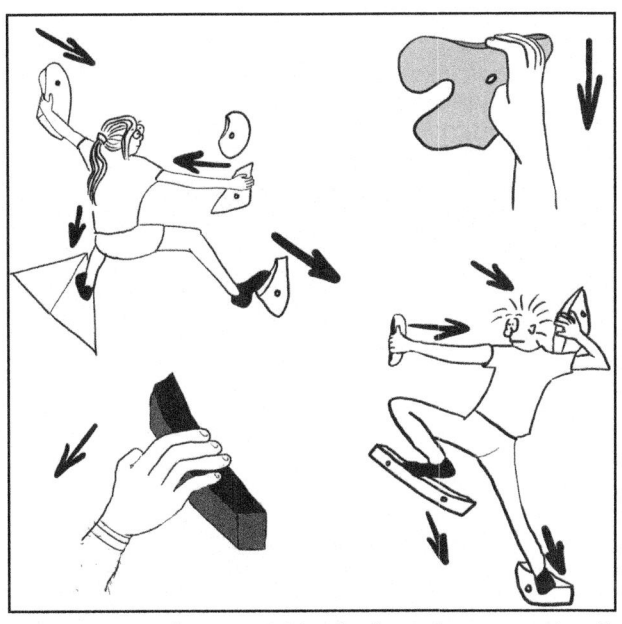

Study each hold and try to determine what would be the best direction of pull, so that you can position your body in the opposite direction, maximising the opposing forces to keep you on the hold.

Some holds will look FABULOUS from the ground, but when you reach them, you'll suddenly realise they're rubbish! It just means you'll have to put in a little more effort than you expected. With any hold, there is likely to be some part that has a slightly better grip, so if the hold doesn't feel that positive initially, try different hand and finger positions or change the angle of your wrist, arm, or body. With a bit of experience you can quickly learn to anticipate what a hold will feel like and how best to position yourself.

(iv)   **I'll be straight with you**

Each time you pull on a hold, your arm muscles engage. The harder you pull and the further you travel, the more tired your arms will become. Exactly how quickly you become tired will depend on a variety of factors, including how strong you are and how much you weigh, but you can dramatically improve your ability for sustained climbing by using straight, rather than bent arms. When your arms are bent your muscles take most of the strain. Consider the fact that those poor muscles must hold your ENTIRE BODY onto the wall. Each time you move from one hold to another they engage and release. Now, my body is heavy at the best of times… especially after eating a cheeseburger meal, chocolate milkshake, and an extra side of lard… so anything I can do to make it easier, the better!

When you straighten your arms, a proportion of your body weight is redistributed to your skeletal system. That means much less stress on your muscles, so they will be better able to cope. Although your arm muscles will still need to be engaged, this will be much less tiring than if there were bent. Straight arm climbing also encourages better use of the movement and strength of your lower body to push you up the wall. Consequently, you will be able to climb longer and harder.

"This is a breeze!"

(v)   **No holds barred**

There are occasions when you may find that you can use the friction between the palm of your hand and the wall itself, rather than a specific hold. This technique is creatively known as PALMING and is particularly effective climbing in a corner, where you can push away from the wall.

As you might expect, it takes a bit of practice and requires confidence. But the simple fact is, if there is sufficient friction and you are applying enough pressure, you will be able to climb a wall or section of wall that otherwise has no decent holds!

The least you need to know

- Different angled walls - including vertical, slab, overhang, roof, or cave - provide different physical challenges.

- Common, identifiable holds include jugs, slopers, crimps, side pulls, gastons, pockets, pinches, undercuts (but not uppercuts), as well as volumes and footholds.

- You can use a hold more efficiently by applying optimal pressure, using all your digits where appropriate, using opposing forces, and keeping your arms straight.

- Palming is a useful technique, particularly when there are no obvious or useful holds to be found.

5

YOU'RE NOT CLIMBING A LADDER: ESSENTIAL TECHNIQUE

Climbing a ladder is a straightforward climbing experience. Each rung is easy to hold or step onto, equally spaced apart, and only goes in one direction… straight up (unless something has gone horribly wrong). Climbing, however, involves using holds that are sometimes easy, sometimes challenging, and sometimes seemingly impossible … they're not equally spaced and, whilst they do, in the main, go upwards, the route can move in any direction over the wall.

There are some ESSENTIAL elements you need to get right from the word "GO!" (that's like NOW by the way) to SUPERCHARGE your journey to becoming a competent and efficient climber. This chapter will address how, as a climber, you should:

1. THINK about the most efficient way to climb a route.
2. MOVE DELIBERATELY AND PRECISELY.
3. BREATHE in a manner that will help you relax and keep your muscles oxygenated.

Be a cat, not a dog…

I have two dogs. I love dogs. If I was ever kidnapped and shackled by an insane scientist who intended to turn me into an animal, and the choice was… cat or dog… I'd go, "Dog" every time…Unless the mad scientist wanted to create an animal with the best approach to rock climbing, then I'd have to say, "Cat". (Bear with me!)

Consider the following scenario:

A family own a dog and a cat. In summer, they both sleep in separate baskets on a patio which overlooks the garden. One day, a pigeon lands at the bottom of the garden and begins scratching around, searching for titbits to eat.

Either the dog or the cat wakes up…

Scenario 1 - The Dog

The dog wakes up first and sees the pigeon.

It **reacts** instantly, every muscle and sinew in its body taut as it leaps three feet out of its basket and, loudly barking, careers across the garden like a homing missile. The only thing in the dog's mind is... 'PIGEON'. It runs in a dead **straight line**, smashing through garden furniture, sending chairs flying. The dog is still barking as the pigeon calmly flutters up onto a nearby fence, out of harm's way.

The dog got so FIRED UP in the moment that it used a lot of energy, is **panting heavily,** and realises that running into several chairs was quite painful. It goes back to its basket and falls into a deep, exhausted sleep, and dreams of one day catching the pigeon.

Scenario 2 - The Cat

The cat wakes up first and sees the pigeon.

The cat doesn't move, but instead observes the pigeon, and thinks about the best route from its basket to the pigeon... without alerting the pigeon or waking the dog...

The cat moves quietly and stealthily. Its body is relaxed. Its mind focused. The cat moves slowly and cautiously at times, more briskly when it thinks it might get spotted. It rests when it needs to, conserving energy. Although the cat is excited by the prospect of reaching the pigeon, it controls its breathing, ensuring a steady flow of oxygen reaches its muscles. The precision of each footfall, turn, and twist makes for an exquisite sequence of movement from its basket to its goal.

The pigeon squarks its last ever squark...

Cat vs dog

If you're thinking, "I literally have no idea what this idiot is talking about," then bear with me a little longer. What I'm NOT asking you to do is:

Chase pigeons.
Sniff a stranger's butt.
Poo in the garden.
Cough up furballs.
Eat animals that you catch in your teeth.
Wee on a lamp post.

What I am asking you to do is **THINK, MOVE DELIBERATELY AND PRECISELY,** and **BREATHE**:

1. Think

Calm down, calm down... I'm not being rude! I know you are a sentient being capable of thought... I'm just saying, the dog doesn't think; it REACTS. It's a simple reaction which essentially boils down to: CATCH THE PIGEON! The cat on the other hand, stays calm and focused, taking its time to plan its route, and moves with purpose.

You have similar options on a climb – you could adopt the DOG MINDSET and try to tear up the route the fastest way possible. If you're lucky, you MIGHT make it to the top... just before your forearms explode. But if you've just launched onto it without second thought, chances are you will miss holds or subtle movements that might ultimately have made the journey easier. For an easy or straightforward climb that approach may be fine, but for every wrong move you make, there is a consequence - energy loss. The harder the route you climb, the more energy you need, so even a little energy loss can have severe consequences.

If you want to progress, then adopt the CAT MINDSET:

THINK before you act. The best time for planning is **before** you start climbing. So, take some time to study the route before you attempt to ascend it. The simplest and most efficient route isn't necessarily a straight line of ascent. Routes will often require the climber to move in many different directions. Think of each route as a puzzle where there may be many, or only one way to climb to the top. Half of the fun of climbing is thinking through the puzzle and unlocking it.

'READING' a route is about looking at the holds from the bottom of the wall to the top and working out the best way of getting up it. And I don't mean just giving it a quick glance and then jumping on board. Look at the holds that you are going to use: each hold is a piece of the puzzle which you need to unlock to move on, so think about how you're going to get from one to another and then onto the next and the next and the next...

Imagine the correct order in which your hands and feet should go as you climb, seeking to identify the sequence that will get you to the top in the most efficient manner.

The better you get at route reading, the fewer mistakes you are likely to make, and therefore the higher the likelihood you won't run out of energy before the top. As you begin to climb, it may turn out that the holds you thought were good are awful (and vice versa), so be prepared to change your game plan. You may want to consider what your 'Plan B' would be in such an eventuality (i.e. think about a different way to move through the holds).

2. Move deliberately and precisely

If you've thought about your route, you will be less likely to dither on the ascent. So, be confident in making the moves you have planned. Some routes, or parts of a route, may require you to move at different speeds: more quickly, such as moving through a physically demanding overhang, or more slowly, such as a slab climb requiring balance. Whatever speed you move, placing your feet and hands in the best position on available holds, will be crucial in determining whether you will climb a route well, or sometimes, at all. So, don't just grab and stomp your way up the wall. Identify the best hold, or spot on a hold, and then deliberately MOVE to it with pinpoint precision.

Remember, whereas the dog ran hell for leather at the pigeon, the cat conserved its energy by resting along its route. Climbing a route isn't a race (well, unless you happen to be speed climbing and then, yes, it absolutely is a race) and let's be clear: hauling your body up a wall can be tough going. So, absolutely try and conserve energy where you can.

"How exactly does one rest halfway up a wall?" I hear you ask...

Well, the best place to rest is on the ground before you start climbing...

Failing that, you can always look forward to resting once you've completed the climb...

And failing that, you can find a position that is less demanding on your body. For example, if there is a good jug on a route that otherwise consists of tiny crimps, then that's the one to aim to have a rest on.

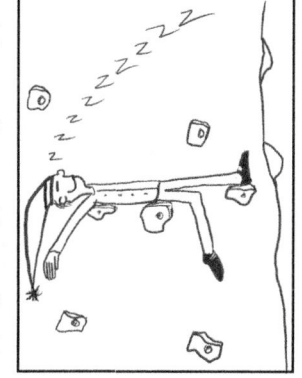

There are some techniques to aid resting on a route described in Chapter 8, The good, the bad and the ugly.

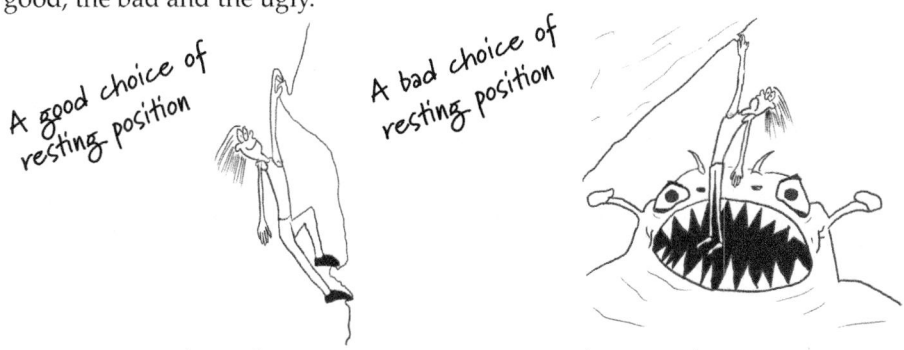

Bear in mind, that whenever your arms are reaching for holds above your head, gravity is working against you. The blood will naturally drain from your arms at a time when your muscles are demanding more oxygen. So, to redress the balance, once you get to a good hold, allow time to dangle one arm beneath your waist. You can also SHAKE OUT tired arms (one at a time, please!) to help get the blood circulating.

The key point to realise is that you need to manage your journey - there will be some parts of a climb that are tougher than others, so finding resting spots along the route will increase your overall chances of completing it altogether.

3. Breathe

I expect if you just picked up this book, opened it to this chapter and read, "Breathe", you'd be like, "I really don't think this book is telling me anything I don't already know!"

But a lot of people have a nasty habit of holding their breath when climbing. That's okay when you're doing a short powerful move, but any longer than a few seconds is counterproductive: climbing is a cardiovascular activity requiring plenty of oxygenated blood to feed the muscles... stop breathing and you starve your muscles... making it harder to climb.

A little better than holding one's breath, but still far from useful, is shallow breathing: it's the kind of breathing you do when you're nervous or anxious, like when you're climbing higher or harder than you're comfortable with. Ironically, it's exactly the type of breathing that makes us even more nervous or anxious and will undoubtedly make the climb more difficult. So, if you're panting like the dog, it's important to try and consciously slow your breathing.

Being aware how you are breathing will help you identify whether you are tense or calm. So, consciously focus on your inhalations and exhalations before and during your climb. Try and maintain steady breathing... even when you are tiring. Whilst this won't always be possible, particularly during hard moves, maintaining awareness of your breath will help you get it back in check. Making a "shushing" noise as you exhale is a really good way of monitoring your breathing as you climb, and you will quickly determine any changes. You want to be relaxed like the cat and taking smooth, controlled breaths. Frankly, "purr" if it helps your focus!

The least you need to know

- **THINK** – Plan your route from the ground before you start climbing. Read the whole route from bottom to top, deciding where you will put your hands and feet. Have a Plan B.

- **MOVE DELIBERATELY AND PRECISELY** – Move through the route you have planned with confidence, taking care to place your hands and feet so that you make best use of each hold. Use opportunities to rest during the ascent.

- **BREATHE** – Focus on the way you are breathing and try to maintain steady breaths, keeping your body relaxed and oxygenated.

- Be a cat, not a dog.

6

BEST FOOT FORWARDS: THE IMPORTANCE OF FOOTWORK

Many climbers mistakenly think that the key to improved climbing is building strong fingers, hands, and arms, to pull themselves up the wall. An element of strength is important, but below your waist are an even larger set of limbs with muscles capable of propelling you upwards... I'm talking about your legs! This chapter will explain:

- The benefit of using your legs whilst climbing.
- The importance of good footwork.
- The different parts of the foot used in climbing.
- The impact of the position of your foot on a hold.
- How to climb without any footholds.

Doing all the legwork

Take a glimpse of the difference between your legs and your arms... most people have much larger leg muscles than their arm muscles. Okay, so there will always be an exception to the rule. But generally, it makes more sense to rely on your legs than your arms because they should have more power, strength, and stamina.

Stand up...

No, don't just read this... stand up... go on, humour me!

Right... now close your eyes...

Actually, read this first before you close your eyes, otherwise you won't know what to do once you've closed your eyes (If you've already closed your eyes before reading this, we're going to have to start all over again):

I want you to concentrate on where you feel your weight is... it should be over your feet. When you close your eyes, you might start to wobble, and you will feel the weight transfer to your toes, heel, or balls of your feet. Stand on one leg and things are going to get a little trickier. I'm guessing you're good at standing on your own two feet so it shouldn't be too tiring; your legs taking the weight of your entire body with relative ease. Standing on just one leg might become a little more tiring, but all in all, it's not going to be GUT-BUSTINGLY difficult.

Now, as a comparison, try holding your body weight using just your hands and arms. You're going to have to hang off something – a wall, door frame, your mate's shoulders (preferably giving them some notice before you do). All I want you to do is lift your feet off the floor and hang there...

Was it difficult?

I'm guessing some of you couldn't hang at all, some could hold themselves up for a short while, and maybe a few could hold themselves there for much, much longer... I'm also guessing at least one person who hung off their mate's shoulders was advised in no uncertain terms to, "Get off!" or words to that effect. Anyway, my point is rather simple: it's a lot easier holding the weight of your body on your legs and feet than it is on your arms and hands. SOOOOOOOOOOO, it follows that climbing will be a lot less tiring if you use your feet and legs to take most of your weight and push yourself up the wall. And to do this, you need to develop good FOOTWORK.

Keep your eye on the ~~ball~~ foot

Okay – wait for it – this is another WORLD CLASS climbing tip which you will be sure to thank me for in years to come: Your feet are key to climbing so, **look where you intend to place your feet**. Do you need to sit down given the magnitude of this revelation (Make sure you look where to sit first)?!

Okay, it might not sound that profound, but it is an important habit to develop. Many, many climbers are so busy looking up for handholds, they forget about their feet altogether. So, look for a good hold and... don't stop there... keep looking as you place your foot on the hold. Which takes me onto my next point:

Precision

You need to place your foot PRECISELY. No point in looking down at your feet if you're going to just stick them anywhere and any-old-how.

You really need to pay attention to exactly where you place your foot on a hold, considering the shape and direction of the hold itself. You want to aim for the area that will provide you with the greatest purchase and stability, making the most of the available space, whilst also considering where you eventually want your foot to push or pull you to. Now, I've said FOOT but, as we're talking about precision, to be PRECISE, there are only certain parts of your foot that you want to be using. If you were clambering up great big jugs, stepping on them any-old-how mightn't necessarily impede your ascent, but trying to squash the wrong part of your size 9's onto a smaller hold is going to be a disaster. The shoe outline identifies the area to use:

White

This part of the foot is a, "GO! GO! GO!" when it comes to climbing. Using the forefront of your foot allows you to easily pivot on a hold and, if required, stand on tiptoes to extend your reach further. Your toes are strong enough to balance on the tiniest edges, and your big toe, literally the 'Hercules' of toes (only less hairy… hopefully), can support your entire body weight.

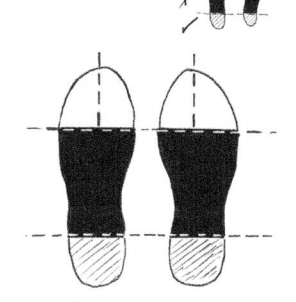

Striped

There are certain moves in climbing where only a heel will do, but you certainly don't want to use them to balance on smaller edges (unless you happen to be in a blockbuster comedy, amusingly side stepping around a window ledge away from some baddies). Rather than stepping on it, your heel can be used to HOOK over a hold and pull your body closer to the wall. We'll go into this in more detail later in Chapter 8, under the catchy heading 'Heel hooks' (I know, I am remarkably creative!).

Shaded

Red light! RED LIGHT! Human feet evolved arches to distribute weight and act as shock absorbers. You don't even WALK on the arches of your feet, so definitely don't climb on them.

On the edge

Foot holds vary in size: some will be bigger than your foot, others seemingly microscopic. The way you place your foot can mean the difference between it being as beneficial as the next rung on a ladder, or as poor as if you were stepping on a LOW HANGING CLOUD! Where a hold is very small, you can just use the EDGE of your climbing shoe to stand on it, a technique otherwise known as… (you've guessed it) 'edging'.

As we now know, the most powerful part of your foot in climbing is THE BIG TOE, so using the inside edge of your foot provides a great deal of stability on smaller holds. Having your foot sideways also opens your hips and gets you closer to the wall. This is important because, generally, the closer you are to the wall, the more your weight will be over your feet, forcing them downwards onto the hold.

To further hook yourself on a hold, pull your toe inwards (like you would use your fingers, pulling you into the wall) at the same time as pushing downwards.

The edges of climbing shoes are made of stiff rubber so you can also use the outside edge of your shoe on holds, particularly if you want to change direction. Using the outer edge is likely to feel a little less sturdy because you will be relying on your smaller toes, but it does also help get your hips close to the wall.

Using the inside of one edge and the outside of another is another great way of getting your hips close to the wall.

If you use the inside edge of each shoe at the same time you can also do a fantastic impression of a lesser-spotted-mountain-frog. Good hip flexibility is key to remaining close to the wall.

However, if you use the outside edge of each shoe at the same time, you probably need to go to the doctor, because your legs shouldn't do that!

If you are new to climbing, you may find it beneficial to adopt a 45-degree foot angle. This gives a good amount of movement potential. As you explore climbing further you can start to unlock the perfect foot angle for each hold or move.

Be advised: the stiffness of the sole of your shoe can have a dramatic effect on your climbing. A stiffer shoe is more likely to line up nicely with a small edge, but if the sole is too rigid, standing on a hold will be more difficult because you won't be able to feel it beneath your foot. Conversely, whilst you may be able to better feel the hold with a softer shoe, it can sometimes feel like you are in danger of rolling off and, if they're really soft, a tiny edge could feel like you're balancing on a razor blade.

Practice challenge:

- Find an easy route.
- Climb it with your feet and body face on.
- Next, climb with your feet facing left (e.g. left hip close to the wall).
- Now climb with your feet facing to the right (e.g. right hip close to the wall).
- Finally, climb placing your feet however feels best to ascend the wall.

This exercise will help you appreciate the impact different foot placement can have to your stability, balance, and movement.

Twist and shout… (Although no need to SHOUT)

When you step on a hold it will often be possible to rotate your foot from one side to another. Rotating your foot in one direction is the start of a TWIST or PIVOT, that includes your knee, hips, and shoulders, turning your body sideways onto the wall so that, rather than climbing face-on to the wall, you will be in a more energy efficient side to side movement.

When your body is sideways, one of your shoulders will be closer to the wall and, as if by magic, you will also find that you have a much longer reach.

When you start climbing with a twist, it can feel a bit unnatural and clunky, so it is well worth trialling your newfound skill on easier routes. This way you should feel more comfortable experimenting twisting and turning, even if you do look like you're doing disco moves on a vertical dance floor!

When the technique is completed correctly, you should also find that you are less likely to **pull** yourself up with your arms, instead relying on the power generated from your hips and legs to **push** yourself up the wall.

But actually, who needs footholds?

SMEARING is an essential climbing technique to help gain as much traction on the surface climbed as possible. It's a full-on Spider-man/woman/person technique for climbing up a wall when you don't have any viable footholds.

Smear Ingredients:

- 2 x good quality climbing shoes.
- 1 x climber.
- 1 x sloping surface, such as (i) rock or (ii) artificial rock (including volumes and large holds).
- 1 x dollop of confidence, mixed with a sprinkling of determination.

Method:

First the climber needs to place a climbing shoe on each foot (it is better to have the right shoe on the right foot, and the left shoe on the left foot). The climber then pushes their foot against the rock with the weight concentrated over the toes and ball of the foot. The aim is to get as much surface contact between the underside of the climbing shoe and the rock surface, so the climber should have a low heel to get as much of the rubber of the shoe on the rock. The climber should look for their next foothold, keeping an eye out for any indentations or protrusions that might aid purchase. Move the other foot up the incline and repeat.

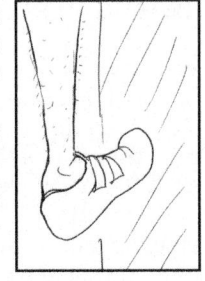

Smearing is a hugely important technique for slab climbing. Grasping the technique is essential to prevent overreliance on inefficient pulling with the arms, rather than pushing with the legs and feet. The relevance of smearing is probably best realised on climbs which lack hand or footholds. There don't tend to be many of these in indoor climbing gyms, whereas outdoors, there are numerous. Climbing anything without the added reassurance of being able to hang on with your hands can be an unnerving experience. But, in plain terms, you walk around all day long without the need to grab onto something, so walking upwards shouldn't be all that unusual, should it?

Whilst slab climbing doesn't tend to rely on the same levels of upper body strength required in ascending a vertical or overhanging climb, it can be more mentally taxing as you literally GET TO GRIPS with trusting that your feet won't slip. I cannot emphasise this enough - the rubber soles of climbing shoes are designed to be good at sticking to surfaces, so place your trust in your feet, and move. The more practice you get the more confident you will become.

Is it a good time to mention 'Disco leg'?

DISCO LEG sounds like something your grandfather would get at a wedding party. But it's the name given to the unpleasant situation when your leg begins to violently wobble on the spot, like a crazed sewing machine. It can occur when your legs are tired (e.g. on a calf busting slab climb) or when you're feeling a little anxious. Fortunately, the best way to stop a wobbly leg is to simply lower your heel. That is, unless you are climbing during an earthquake, where dropping your heel is unlikely to make much difference.

Foot swap

You'll be relieved to know there should never be a requirement for you to get a completely new set of feet for climbing, but being able to SWAP YOUR FEET on a hold may be useful.

You might find that you have your left foot on a hold that you want to use for your right; and vice versa.
Realise that you MAY be in this position because you read the route incorrectly (particularly if you're me). Learning an efficient way to swap feet is important

if you need to get yourself out of difficulty!

Swapping your feet needn't be overly complicated. If there's enough room on the hold, you can simply place one foot next to the other and then take the first foot off. If there is insufficient room for two feet on the hold, you can instead hop from one foot to another. It's not going to be an easy move to pull off on a small hold though and, if you miss, you're going to suddenly strain your arms to stop yourself slipping off the wall altogether. A more controlled swap can be achieved by rolling one foot off the hold at the same time as you roll your other foot on it.

When you're nudging one foot onto a hold at the same time as moving the other off you begin to realise the importance of precision footwork. Try to move your foot onto the hold sideways rather than stepping down on top of your other foot. It would be the equivalent of standing on your own foot and trying to walk… it doesn't work!

"This hold ain't big enough for the both of us!"

Foot loose but not fancy free

Imagine you are confidently climbing on the wall, ascending a route without a care in the world, when you step out to a foothold and SLIP!

Slipping on a hold can be a horrible experience…

You might slip right off the wall altogether, or save yourself, your arms suddenly having to take the weight of your body. If you're unlucky, the sudden jolt will lead to hand or finger injury. It's no wonder many climbers get nervous when attempting to step on small or sloped holds. But THINK: if you slipped in the street, it's likely that you'd experience some anxiety (particularly if you'd slipped on a MASSIVE DOG POO), so it's quite natural to experience some anxiety if you do slip on a climb.

Slips generally occur because one's foot is misplaced on a hold (e.g. the climber misses it) or the foot isn't sufficiently stable on the hold and slides off. The GREAT NEWS is the solution is straightforward:

- Make sure your shoes are done up and **fit snugly**. Any foot slippage within an ill-fitted shoe will negatively impact your footwork per se.

- **Clean your shoes!** You want the specialised rubber sole of your climbing shoe sticking itself to the surface of each hold. Anything that compromises the two surfaces, including chalk dust, will leave you with less friction and a higher likelihood of a slip. So, rub the soles of your shoes clean, concentrating particularly on the shoe box (toe area). Many climbers carry a little towel for just this occasion, wiping their shoes on it before they climb. You can also consider a good ole fashioned 'spit and shine': that is to say, spit on the bottom of your shoe, rub it clean of any filth and wipe it dry on your towel/shirt/friend (delete as appropriate) before you start your route.

- Don't just stop with your shoes. Excess chalk can build up on holds so it's always worthwhile giving the holds a clean. Get yourself a good boulder brush and give whatever hold or surface that's got you worried a good rub down.

- As highlighted earlier in the chapter, **look where you intend to place your feet** - this will certainly help reduce the likelihood of missing the hold altogether and ensure that you place your foot precisely on the best part of the hold, rather than a point that has less purchase.

- Repeat the mantra, "**A weighted foot never slips**". The more pressure bearing down on a hold, the less likely there will be any movement. The weight of your own body can literally hold you on a hold. Where possible, smoothly transition your weight from one hold to another, and think about direction – if you can pull into a hold rather than away from it - this will help. It is very much a question of TRUST.

When you begin climbing, it's difficult to imagine standing on anything smaller than your foot would support you, let alone anything smaller than your big toe. But even the teeniest, bumps, or grooves in the rock can support a person. The internet is awash with videos of some of the best climbers ascending walls more akin to sheets of glass than rock. I'm not saying that once you start climbing, you're going to be able to balance on a pimple on a gnat's butt, but the more you try and place your trust in your footing, what might once have been seemingly impossible sized holds will transform into a stairway to heaven.

Low down traversing on gradually smaller holds is a great way of gaining confidence before moving your way up the wall. So, practice, practice, practice!

The least you need to know

- Use the strong muscles in your legs to push you up the wall.

- Look where you intend to place your feet.

- **Stand on holds using your toes rather than your whole foot, and use the inside and outside edge of your shoe.**

- You can pivot or swap feet on a hold.

- **In the absence of holds, keep a low heel and smear up the climbing surface.**

- **To reduce your chances of slipping: wear well-fitted, clean shoes, move precisely, transitioning your weight smoothly between holds, and keep each foot weighted.**

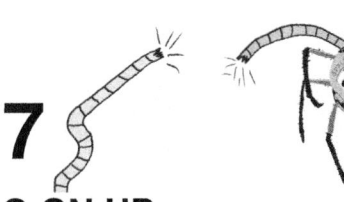

7
MOVING ON UP: GRAVITY, BODY POSITION, AND MOVEMENT

Although we are all physically different, there are some fundamental elements in climbing that everyone can influence to their advantage. Changing the position of your body in relation to the wall and the way you move will dramatically impact your ability to climb. This chapter will provide an understanding of:

- The impact of gravity on your climbing.
- How to use your legs for balance (flagging).
- Dynamic versus static movement.
- How to jump or 'dyno' between holds.

You versus gravity

As I'm sure you're already aware, according to Albert Einstein's theory of relativity, "gravity is a consequence of the curvature of space-time caused by the uneven distribution of mass..."

I know... OBVIOUS right?!

All day, everyday, gravity pulls on your whole body. If it didn't, you'd float off into space (which might sound nice, except that space is very cold, dark, and has few decent restaurants). And unless you happen to be an astronaut circling the moon or a bizarre alien species living in a weightless zone of the universe, gravity is going to play hell with your climbing! The weight of your own body is going to drag you off the wall. You have a couple of options:

Option 1: Defy gravity. Possible if you happen to be superhuman with a skill set involving flying. However, if you are superhuman with a skill set involving flying, why are you bothering climbing exactly?!

Option 2: Move and position your body in such a way that the INEVITABLE forces of gravity take less of a toll...

Assuming you are going with option 2, there are some key things you can do from the moment you start climbing to make you more efficient:

> "In the blue corner weighing in at 80 kg is 'the author', and in the red corner, the invisible force that pulls objects towards each other and undisputed champion of the Universe: 'The Earth's Gravity'...
>
> Bets are on –
>
> Infinity:1 Earth's Gravity to win every time for eternity"

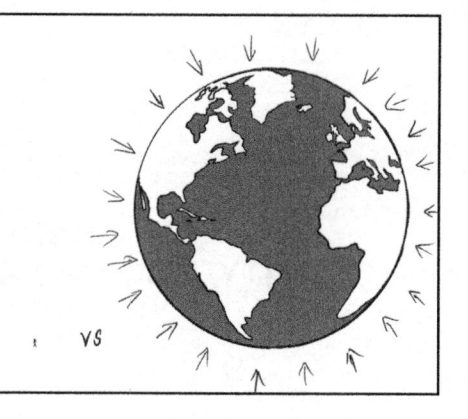

Think about your body position

The spot in your body where that 'pull' or weight is concentrated the most is called the CENTRE OF GRAVITY. Any guesses as to where it usually is? Yes… in the CENTRE of your body. So, if you're standing up on two legs your centre of gravity will be generally just below your belly button.

To help grasp the concept of how gravity affects your climbing, it's useful to think of it like having a heavy weight strapped around your waist. The weight will be constantly pulling towards the ground.

Generally, if you keep close to the wall, the weight will hang over your feet, pushing them down onto the holds and providing stability. Lean out from the wall and that weight moves out too, pulling you away from the footholds and off the wall altogether. So, from the very start of a vertical or overhanging climb, pull yourself close to the wall and keep close throughout.

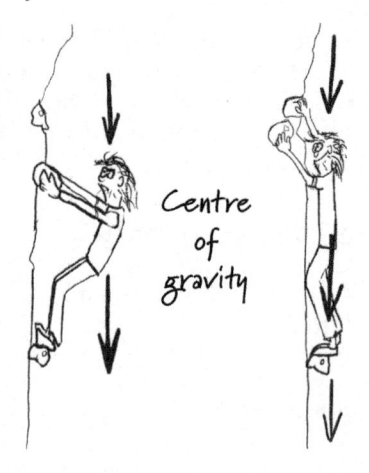

In the case of climbing a slab, the situation is slightly different. If you pull your body close to the wall, your centre of gravity may be too far forward and with less weight / gravitational force pushing down on your feet, they could slip from under you. To prevent this you want your centre of gravity in line with your feet, so that the weight pushes down on the climbing surface.

If you're super keen, you can work out where your centre of gravity is whilst climbing by using a PLUMB LINE (don't worry - no plums will be harmed during this experiment!). A plumb line is basically a weight suspended from a string and you can make one… by hanging a weight from a string!

Genius heh? Plumb lines are often used by people doing a bit of DIY wallpaper hanging (the plumb line will show if your wallpaper is straight because the weight pulls the string exactly vertical). In our DIY 'find your centre of gravity' you should attach the plumb line around your waist. When you stand with your legs apart, the plumb line will hang straight down between your legs. When you move, your centre of gravity will change, as will the position of the pumb line

"It's as if some invisible force is dragging me off the wall!"

(I would recommend trying this low to the ground because climbing with an extra weight dangling off you is an acccident waiting to happen!).

Rockover

A key climbing technique, that involves transferring your centre of gravity from one foot towards the other, is a ROCKOVER. If you have ever walked up a step or got out of a chair, then a rockover is within your grasp!

Centre of gravity transfer

Rockovers are particularly useful if you're standing on footholds that are wide apart and you want to move, without coming off balance or putting too much strain on your arms. When your weight is balanced on both legs in a wide stance, it can be difficult to lift either leg. Moving your weight over one supporting leg, however, makes it easier to lift the other (and then place it onto the next hold). You simply need to ROCK your weight from one foot OVER to the other, using momentum to bounce between the two.

'Mad Dog' demonstrates undertaking a rockover to avoid a bullet, before slaying his foe...

Practice makes perfect, so try on a variety of holds until you become accustomed to how much momentum is required to carry you from one foot to another. Too little momentum and you won't stick the hold, too much and you'll reach the foothold and carry on going. Remember to drive with your legs, aiming to get you centre of gravity (BELLYBUTTON) over the top of the leg you are rocking over to. You can use your hands to (a) pull yourself in the direction of travel and (b) help stop yourself if your body decides to continue on a trajectory past your intended hold!

Flagging (I don't blame you… it's a lot to take in!)

Ever tried tightrope walking or slacklining? (I only ask because you're adventurous enough to have bought a book on rock climbing). Both involve walking across a piece of material (rope, wire, or webbing) suspended above the ground. You don't have to have worked in the circus to appreciate that anyone involved in such an activity will tend to hold their arms out sideways to help with their balance and, during a wobble, may also put their leg out. The weight of their arms and legs helps to counterbalance the body from tipping one way or another.

In climbing, FLAGGING works on the same principles. It is an incredibly versatile technique to help balance your body, simply by moving one of your legs out to the side, and thereby counteracting the forces of gravity. It really comes into its own when you are using holds on one side of the body.

If you're trying to walk on a tightrope and your weight is on one side, you're going to fall off in that direction. When your weight is on one side in climbing, you will tend to swing out from the wall in an arch, a phenomenon known as BARN DOORING (yeah, I know... dunne sond lik gud englis dos it?).

Barn doors, like most doors on a hinge, swing to the side to open. This is the same motion your body can take when off balance. Simply lifting your leg out to the side of your body will help counteract the swing.

Generally, if you are reaching for a hold on the left, you should flag on your right; and vice versa. You can move your leg in front or behind your supporting leg. There's no doubt, flagging can look and feel odd - crossing your legs over whilst halfway up a wall - but it can work MAGIC, balancing your body, so it's worth investing some time practising and applying in situations when you need to achieve equilibrium.

Static VS Dynamic movement

'Static movement' sounds like a contradiction in terms... I mean, you can't be static if you're moving (e.g. climbing); can you?

Well, STATIC CLIMBING refers to a slow, methodical ascent, the climber moving their body in a very controlled and deliberate fashion. I always tend to climb more statically when I'm a feeling a bit nervous: I absolutely want to ensure that I have a precise grip on each hold so I overcompensate and slooooowwwww riiigghtt doooown...

Sometimes however, you will come across moves that are dang near impossible to do statically, and this is where a climber needs to get DYNAMIC. Dynamic climbing involves the use of MOMENTUM. In the simplest terms you need to jump, 'pop', or lunge for a hold, something which requires accuracy in terms of timing and coordination.

A great way to gain understanding of the use of momentum in climbing is to perform a very simple exercise, ideally on holds close to the ground... it's not as far to fall if you get it wrong:

- Make sure you have four points of contact on the wall (i.e. have each hand on a different hold and each foot on a different hold... Actually, I should have just said that).

- Pull yourself forward towards the wall and instantly release both hands from the holds, clapping them together, before replacing them back on the same holds.

Why?!

Good question. What you SHOULD find is, that as you purposefully throw your chest towards the wall, there will be a MOMENT OF WEIGHTLESSNESS within which you can clap your hands, before gravity pulls you backwards. You are halfway to becoming a ninja. Feel free to insist people call you "Grand Master" when addressing you from here on in...

Ninja outfit is compulsory

Once you've practiced with both hands going to the same holds, move both hands to different holds. Just reading about it won't 'cut the mustard'. You need to practice. This will help you better understand how much momentum you require to accurately move between the positions.

Pull with your arms
Keep your core tight
Push with your legs
Press down with your feet

That split second moment, when a climber is at the peak end of momentum upwards to a hold, is often referred to as the DEADPOINT.

The perfect dynamic climber generates just enough momentum to reach the target hold. Anything more would be a waste of energy. Anything less... well, you aren't going to reach your target destination!

Basically, dynamic climbing makes it is possible to reach holds that are further away, quicker, and with less energy expenditure.

It's not as if one type of climbing is necessarily any better than the other - an ability to move seamlessly between styles would be optimal. The type of route will often dictate what style you can use. For example, there is little need for any dynamic movement when climbing a slab, because slab climbing generally requires balance and precision (i.e. better achieved through static climbing). Conversely, a static technique may not be appropriate for a really 'reachy' overhang, when you want to be firing up it using as little energy as possible, quick as a RAT UP A DRAINPIPE.

Perhaps the ultimate dynamic move is...

The 'DYNO'

A dyno is the explosive movement of dynamically jumping to a hold, where you effectively launch yourself from one set of holds, fly through the air (in a controlled manner!), before latching onto your target hold.

"A-I-R-B-O-R-N-E!!!"

The alternative dyno

This is where accuracy is crucial:

Launch too far and you might sail past the target hold...

Not enough power and you'll fall short of the target hold...

Ever tried seeing how far you can jump from one spot to another? Likelihood is that you crouched down first, spring loading your legs, before driving upwards/forwards.

The same concept applies with the dyno: where possible, take a moment to spring load your legs, crouching down in the hold, before launch. Some people like to pump up and down a couple of times, readying themselves for the launch. Do whatever you feel comfortable with.

Only thing I would avoid doing is a countdown... at least not from 10... maybe start at 3! Fix your eyes on the target hold, and in one, strong, fluid motion straighten your legs and pull down with your arms at the same time, driving your body in your intended direction.

Launching from a set of holds into the air takes confidence. Your brain has been relying on using the holds, dips, dimples, grooves, and cracks on a wall to keep you attached to it, and suddenly you're launching yourself off the wall altogether! But practising dynamic movement per se should help prepare your body and, perhaps more importantly, your mind to fully commit to the movement. If you're anything like me trying a dyno for the first time, you'll be like a malfunctioning rocket launcher shooting off in all directions. It's such an EXPLOSIVE move that it can take time to get the right momentum, trajectory, and timing.

Indoor bouldering gyms typically have a lot of dyno problems, mainly because they're a lot of fun and, if you catch them right, you'll feel like a movie action hero, diving to safety from a raging fire, hail of bullets, or hideous monster.

However, if you don't catch them right you risk sailing into the wall or someone else, so it's super important to think about your trajectory and your likely landing zone... and then CLEAR THE AREA.

Landing the hold also takes practice....

When you dyno, your feet and hands come completely off the holds. Although your hands will be able to grip the next hold, your feet can't (unless you happen to have been born on the 'Planet of the Apes'). Your fingers, hands, and arms are going to act as brakes, so that you STOP on the hold. Your feet and legs, however, are going to continue along the same trajectory, and risk hitting the wall or pull you off the hold completely.

The best way to reduce swing is having good core strength (cue – sit-ups, plank, and other stomach crunching exercises - HATED by millions, don't seem to have anything to do with climbing, and yet, are surprisingly key), but don't be afraid to lift your feet up and plant them on the wall to stop yourself.

Whilst theoretically you can dyno to any hold you want, you are basically trying to latch onto a hold at speed, which can, in that instant put a tremendous load on your arms and, not least, your fingers.

Also, be advised: when you're trying to grip a hold on the move, your skin isn't going to like it. Even repeated attempts on a man-made indoor climbing hold can tear and damage your skin. In general, to avoid injury, don't dyno onto small or awkwardly shaped holds. If in doubt, check out the hold first – hang off it is necessary – better to be prepared rather than spend a week, month, or even longer off because you overdid it on one move.

The least you need to know

- Being aware of your centre of gravity will help you to appreciate where your body should be in relation to the wall.

- Generally, on a vertical or overhanging wall, your centre of gravity wants to be as close to the wall as possible, whilst on a slab climb, your centre of gravity should be set back away from the wall and directly over your feet.

- A rockover involves the use of momentum to transfer your weight from one foot to the other.

- Flagging enables a climber to counterbalance the forces of gravity, using the weight of their outstretched leg to maintain balance and stay on the wall.

- Static climbing involves slow controlled movements. Dynamic climbing involves the use of momentum to spring between holds.

- A dyno requires confidence, accuracy, and explosive movement. For success, establish your trajectory and ensure you fully commit to the move.

8

THE GOOD, THE BAD, AND THE UGLY: MORE ON TECHNIQUE

There's a host of commonly recognised climbing 'moves' that aren't easily categorised but are essential in specific climbing situations. This chapter describes a how to execute each move and when to apply them, including:

- Laybacking.
- Bridging / stemming.
- Chimneying.
- Drop knees.
- Knee bars.
- Heel and toe hooks.
- Bat hangs.
- Lock-offs.
- Mantling /Mantleshelfing.

Opposites attract (the power of opposing forces...)

The layback

LAY-BACKING sounds relaxing, doesn't it?

"Yeah... laying back in the meadow and chewing on a piece of straw; just chilling out in the hot sun..."

WRONG! It's an incredibly strenuous series of moves that allows you to progress up a vertical edge or ridge (often referred to as an arête in climbing terminology). It requires a climber to pull with their arms and push with their feet at the same time, with little ability to rest on holds.

It's the opposing forces of these movements that holds the climber to the wall. It is physically demanding just to hold yourself in the layback position, but moving requires considerable strength and a pinch of good ole fashioned GUTS, because any loss of body tension will result in a fall.

To master the technique: as you move a hand, there needs to be an increase in pressure in your feet, and vice versa when you replace your hand and move your feet up. Keep your arms straight and drive outward with your feet, so you are opposing the inward pull of the arms. It can feel like a slightly unnerving shuffle up the wall, but the more practice you get the more swiftly and confidently you will move.

Chimneying

To CHIMNEY requires a climber to push with their hands, feet, back, and even butt, to squeeze their way up a climb between two walls. I guess you could use the technique to climb the inside of a chimney if you really wanted to, presumably when the fire wasn't lit. Basically, it is a method of climbing that, once again, relies on using counterforce to keep you in place. I've found that it's best started by laying my back against one wall and then pushing one foot against the opposite wall, before swiftly placing my other foot against the same side that my back is leaning on. You must exert opposing pressure, so PUSH your legs in opposite directions IMMEDIATELY. Any loss of pressure and you are only going one way, and that is...

D
O
W
N

To move upwards, you want to place the palms of your hands on opposite walls and PUSH your arms in opposite directions (i.e. exert opposing pressure). Then, draw your back slightly away from the wall whilst straightening your legs. As soon as you've moved up a notch, you need to swiftly reapply pressure from your legs and push your back, back against the wall. Continue this sequence of movements to ascend. Believe me - you're not going to move very far each transition - it pretty much depends on the width of the chimney, the difference in length of your bent to a straight leg, and how far you think you can move without losing grip!

Father Xmas demonstrates the reverse chimney

You're unlikely to do much in the way of chimneying in a climbing gym, but outdoor climbing provides a huge variety of different vertical fissures, or crevices, in the rock upon which to hone your new-found talent.

Even if you're not ready for the outdoor rock experience, I've found a good way of practicing this technique whilst walking my dogs. Every so often, we will come across two trees standing next to each other at which point, much to the dogs' confusion, I shuffle my way up the gap as far as I can muster. It's a great way of perfecting your chimneying technique on a variety of different sized gaps, although other walkers will think you are a lunatic.

Drop knee

No, it's not a leg disorder. The DROP KNEE is yet another technique which relies on oppositional forces – this time just between your feet. The technique can be useful when climbing steep walls or when holds are just out of reach. If you are aiming to reach a hold with your LEFT HAND, then you will need to drop knee your LEFT LEG:

- With your right foot firmly on a hold, step high with the left and swivel your foot on the hold so that your knee turns inwards and downwards – like you're trying to kneel on one leg in mid-air.
- The weight should be on the outside of the 'drop knee-ed foot', as you bridge between it and your other foot.
- The opposing position of your right foot on one hold and your (somewhat bizarrely positioned) left foot provide the tension to hold you to the wall.
- Now, swing your left hip towards the wall and, with a straight arm, reach your left hand to the next hold.
- The fact that your knee is out of the way means you should be able to get your hips a lot closer to the wall and, consequently, your reach will be longer.

The principles of the drop knee are the same on both legs (assuming you have two), so if you are aiming to reach a hold with your RIGHT HAND, you'll need to drop knee with your RIGHT LEG. It's better to move the dropped knee foot 2nd because it can be placed more accurately. Make sure you leave enough space on the foothold for the foot to pivot as you drop the knee. Caution must be taken when using the drop knee as it can place considerable strain on the muscles, tendons, and ligaments of the knee. So, make sure you are warmed up, and only hold the position for as long as is necessary.

Take a rest enroute

Climbing is a tiring business and, whilst you may be able to hang by your arms and take a quick breather, there are a couple of useful techniques that, used in the right situation, can provide a complete break from the ascent altogether:

Mind the gap (Bridging/stemming)

BRIDGING, otherwise known as STEMMING, is a technique you'll find invaluable climbing in a corner. It simply requires you to straddle the holds on either wall, or, if you're brave, smearing on either side.

By pressing your feet on opposing walls you can take a significant amount of weight off your arms and, if you find a secure spot, you can even take your hands off altogether.

Knee bar

A knee bar makes essential use of the one part of your body that you wouldn't normally think of as crucial to holding you on the wall; your:

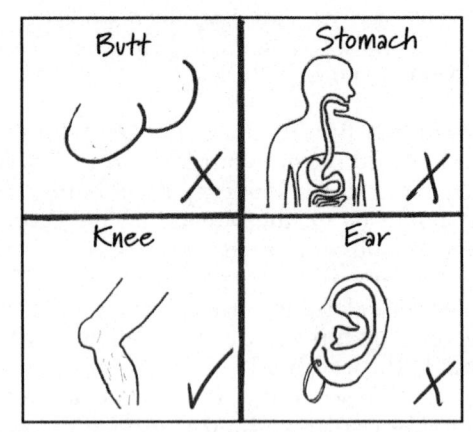

Butt ✗	Stomach ✗
Knee ✓	Ear ✗

Finding a knee bar is akin to discovering an oasis in the desert. Knee bars are few and far between, and it requires a keen eye to spot them. If you do find one however, it can be an absolute life saver (well… energy saver).

A knee bar is achieved when you have your foot on one hold and then squeeze, wedge, or lock your bent knee under another nearby hold or surface. Being locked into knee bar allows you to utilise small or 'bad' holds that you would not otherwise have been able to hold. It also provides a fantastic opportunity to take a rest on a climb. In fact, a good knee bar may even allow the bravest/daftest/most confident to completely let go with their arms and rely solely on the knee bar.

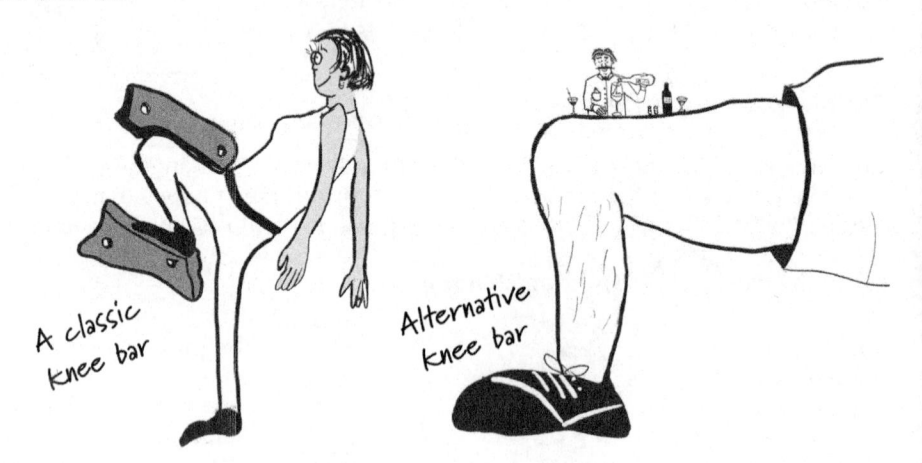

A classic knee bar

Alternative knee bar

The knee bar relies on oppositional forces between your foot and knee, so as with any climbing technique involving oppositional force, you need to maintain tension (e.g. keep your leg tense!) or you'll slip right out of the hold… and, if you had let go with your arms, everyone will agree you deserved it for being a know-it-all show-off!

Jab - jab - right hook, left hook, heel hook, toe hook...

Okay... so you don't just use your feet to delicately balance on holds. There are times when you can use parts of your foot to pull your body closer to the wall, taking the weight off your arms and helping maintain body tension.

Heel hooks

So, first things first – before you even attempt a heel hook – make sure your shoes are done up tight. I'm always getting reprimanded for kicking my everyday shoes off without undoing the laces... but when the laces are done up tight, I can't get the suckers off.

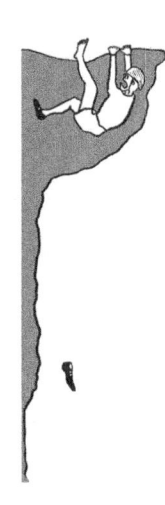

Apply the same rule: you're going to be pulling your heel against a hold, and the last thing you want is your shoe popping off when you're halfway up the wall... or even worse... at the top. So heed my advice and tie the laces/pull the Velcro strap tight.

A heel hook uses the giant leg muscles in your leg and so, when you do it right, it's an amazingly strong technique that is going to pull your body close to the wall and allow you to remain completely stable as you reach for the next hold. As with all footwork, it's important to look for the best place on a hold to execute the heel hook, making the most of any lumps, bumps, dips, or dimples. Once you identify a hold to use a heel hook on, let's be clear, you're not using it as a footrest – HOOK your heel around the hold. You can lock it in place by pulling your heel towards your butt... and when I say pull, I mean PULL HARD!

If you're doing it right, your legs muscles, especially your hamstrings and calf muscles, will be taut with the exertion. Pointing your toes can help ACTIVATE your leg. If you don't pull hard enough, then the likelihood is your foot will slip off the hold, so tense your core and PUUUUUUUUUUUULLLLLLLLLLLLLL!

In fact, continue pulling as you reach for the next hold. All that effort is going to clamp you to the wall, stabilising your body, and allowing you to gain purchase on the next hold with confidence.

Toe hooks

Toe hooks are similar to heel hooks, but just using your ear... Not really!

Rather than balancing on your tootsies, instead you're going to use the top of your toes to hook around a hold, corner, or edge of a wall. The principles of a toe hook are the same as a heel hook – you can pull yourself closer to the wall, maintain stability, and relieve some of the pressure from your arms.

This time you're going to place the top of your foot behind the hold and pull away from it by flexing your shin, hips, and core. You're aiming for a 90-degree angle between the top of your foot and your leg.

So how do you choose when to use a heel hook rather than a toe hook, or vice versa? In many cases, the terrain is going to dictate which would be best, but it will also come down to how flexible you are, how strong your specific leg muscles are, and your confidence using each technique.

Heel hooks are especially powerful, and therefore useful, when climbing steep overhangs. Toe hooks are very good for maintaining one's balance, particularly good on arêtes, or where you really need to stretch for a hold.

A key point to remember for both techniques however, is that it's super important to maintain tension in the leg that is doing the hooking. There is no time to relax – a drop in tension/pressure will soon earn you the title of "Slippy McSlipfoot".

Also, bear in mind that the hook is holding you in place, so as you release it, your body is going to want to swing in the opposite direction, potentially pulling you off the wall. Help prevent this happening by placing your other foot on the best nearby hold that money can buy, tense your core, and have a good grip with your hands.

Captain Hook's lesser known acquaintance, Mid-Shipman Hook...

Bat hang

Hanging like a bat is not a very common climbing move, other than particularly demanding boulder routes, and comes with an element of risk (you're hanging upside-down... and you're not a bat!), so caution needs to be applied when attempting it.

The bat hang is the ultimate, two-footed toe hook. You're going to want a large hold to comfortably get both feet on, and ideally something that is flat. To execute one, you need to place the area of your foot just above your toes onto the hold. You will be relying on the weight of your body pulling your feet down onto the hold (just the opposite side to normal!). To maximise grip on the hold, its best to pull your toes towards your knees, aiming to get your feet at least 90-degrees, with your legs and ankles rigid with tension.

Once you attain the position, it's a perfect opportunity for photographic evidence of what a mad-cap, crazy climber you are. But if you need to move from the position (which is generally the idea after all), maintain the rigidity in your legs, ankles, and feet and move slowly and carefully – dude, you're balancing on the tops of your shoes; any sudden movements and you're likely to fall directly on your bonce!

"Think you're cool don't you... but you just wait until you need to go to the toilet!"

The lock-off

So, throughout the book you will have been encouraged to keep your arms straight when climbing. There's always an exception to the rule, and here it is: the LOCK-OFF! A lock-off is a technique that requires a BENT ARM. It's a very static, yet precise means of moving, and useful in situations when you absolutely want to be sure you will reach the next hold in a controlled manner.

The move itself is relatively simple: grip a hold with one hand, your arm fixed at 90-degrees. Hold that position whilst you reach for your next hold with the other arm. Be aware of your elbows sticking outwards - you are not practicing being a chicken. Instead, try and keep your elbow downwards and in line with your hand.

The lock-off requires considerable strength from the shoulder and elbow, but once held it gives you the opportunity to reach out with the other arm with a little more care and precision than normal. You do forfeit a lot of energy with such a move so use it when you need to, such as moving to smaller or difficult to grip holds. Overuse injuries are a common complaint amongst climbers who have overloaded the elbow joint, so again, use sparingly.

Mantling/Mantleshelfing

Search up the definition of a 'mantel' and you will invariably find it described as the shelf above a fireplace; you know, where Great Aunt McPoodigle has a vase containing Great Uncle McPoodigle? No? Well, not to worry. I raise it simply because mantling or mantelshelfing (a shelf for a mantel) is the specific term given to a climbing technique to get on top of a ledge without the use of handholds... RANDOM!

As it happens you will have used a mantelshelf technique in everyday life should you have ever clambered on top of a wall or out of a swimming pool. It's basically climbing onto anything which has a ledge, be it an indoor 'top

The origin of mantleshelfing?

out' boulder (i.e. one that you climb on top of), or an actual ledge on a cliff face. Whilst it's not necessarily a difficult technique, it is one that people often struggle with because it doesn't involve the use of holds and requires more pushing (chest, shoulders, and triceps) than pulling (back, biceps, and forearms) than 'normal climbing' (if there is such a thing!). It takes a bit of practice and it's a good idea to start on something easy (like clambering on top of a wall or out of a swimming pool!!!).

Stage 1 - Reach for the edge of the ledge with both hands and, at the same time, get your feet as high as possible...

Stage 2 - Next, heave your body upwards, pushing with your palms and locking your elbows. It may help to turn one palm around so that your fingers are facing your body.

Stage 3 - Bring one foot (or heel) onto the ledge close to your hands and then rockover it and stand up.

I find the last move by far the hardest... not only is it physically demanding, transferring your weight on to your leg and then standing up, but throw in the added psychological pressure of balancing on the edge of a ledge with no hand holds, and the mantelshelf can induce a bit of anxiety (and the last thing you want is SWEATY PALMS!) I have added Stage 3A, my ALTERNATIVE ENDING, which is, frankly, NOT the technique we are seeking here, but if all else fails its worth a go:

Stage 3A – In the event of stage 3 failure, use your feet to push jolt/throw/launch your upper body onto the ledge. Try and shuffle as much as your torso onto the ledge and then swing your leg up at the earliest opportunity. Drag your body forwards, using all available friction and as much momentum as you can generate! I have no doubt you will be flapping and lurching around like a giant crazed seal, but it's better than falling off (just)!

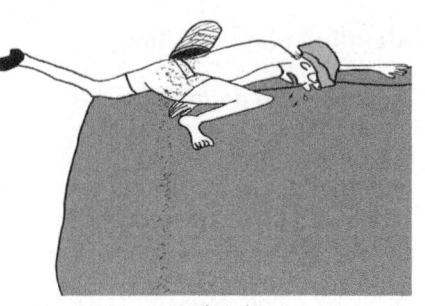

Warning: Not Pretty!

Bear in mind that mantels are often at the TOP of a climb, when you could be at your most tired, so if you know ones coming try and conserve energy before going for it. And make sure your hands are chalked, because you're going to want all the friction you can get for a Stage 3, or worst case a Stage 3A finish!

The least you need to know

- Laybacking, chimneying, and drop knees are techniques utilising the benefit of opposing forces, the simultaneous push and pull locking the climber onto the wall.

- Bridging/stemming and the knee bar offer a fantastic opportunity to rest on a climb, reducing the strain on a climber's arms and providing time to recuperate.

- You can use heel and toe hooks to pull your body close to the wall, help maintain stability, as well as relieve your arms. A bat hang can be performed using a double toe hook. It's important to maintain tension in your legs whilst engaged in any hook.

- A lock-off is an energy sapping but precise method of reaching the next hold in a controlled manner, with a bent rather than straight arm.

- Mantleshelfing is a technique requiring the climber to push their body up and over a ledge or on top of a boulder. It requires strength, commitment and, sometimes, the ability to frantically shuffle forwards on your belly like a seal.

9

I'LL SHOW YOU THE ROPES: A GUIDE TO TOP ROPE CLIMBING INDOORS

In indoor bouldering, climbers ascend short routes and then climb down, jump, or as is often in my case, fall onto the soft matting below. But unless you're accomplished at diving off a crane into a teacup, there comes a point when you ought to realise you could climb to such a height that:

(1) If you did fall there's a chance you're going to miss the matting.
(2) The matting isn't going to protect you even if you did land on it.

Indoor rock gyms don't tend to have any matting in the rope climbing areas. That is because rope climbing allows you to climb with the confidence that if you did fall, you're not going fall the entire length of the wall you just climbed and you're certainly not going to land on the floor! This chapter will provide you with a good understanding of the fundamental requirements of top rope climbing including:

- How to safely 'tie-in' (connect) yourself to the rope.
- Essential belaying tips.
- Rope climbing route grading systems.
- Commonly used communication terms.
- Use of the automatic belay.

The importance of rope

"Don't fail me now boulder mat!"

So, let's get one thing straight before we continue: when I say ROPE, I'm not talking about some tatty bit of string you found at the back of the garage, or the scabby piece tied to a tree branch that local kids use as a swing. I'm talking about immensely strong, vigorously safety tested, climbing specific SAFETY ROPE (see the next chapter on essential equipment under the cunningly entitled subheading, 'Rope' for more detail).

Unless you weigh more than an average car, you do not need to worry... at all... about whether, "the rope is strong enough to hold me". That rope could hold a rhino... carrying heavy weights. It's "GOT YOUR BACK", front, and the rest of you.

Once you get this into your head, you need to address a second crucial point: Rope climbing relies on the introduction of another person to the climbing equation – the BELAYER. The belayer plays a critical role in CONTROLLING THE SAFETY ROPE that connects a climber to the wall. It's important to grasp the following simple dynamic. Consider you were climbing high up a wall. If you slipped and fell and:

a) Didn't have a rope - you'd fall and splat on the floor.

b) Had a rope without a belayer - you'd fall and splat on the floor... with a rope tied to you.

c) Had a rope with a competent belayer – you'd fall and be instantly caught and safely held in the air without any risk of harm.

Okay, so assuming you like the idea of OPTION C... how is the belayer 'catching' you exactly?

"Elementary my dear Watson:

The rugged climber is attached to a sturdy rope. The solid and dependable belayer is also attached to that same sturdy rope, and finally, the rope itself is attached to whatever wall these exploratory fellows are seeking to scale. By way of further explanation, let's talk about probably the safest and easiest way to learn to climb with ropes... TOP ROPING...

Although without the need to continue the pretence that this lesson is being taught by the greatest fictional Victorian Detective in all of London..."

Top roping

Top roping refers to a system of climbing where the rope that is tied to the climber runs through a fixed point at the TOP of the route, with the belayer belaying from the BOTTOM of the route. Rather confusingly, some people also refer to this method as 'bottom roping', a term which I think sounds a bit suspicious! As it happens, bottom roping is the correct term, but it's no longer used except by old farts like me... Let's just stick with top roping to avoid any confusion!

"I was bottom roping officer..."

"You're nicked you fiend!"

Climbing gyms with roofs high enough for rope climbing generally have numerous routes set up for top roping. Normally, standardised safety ropes are affixed to the wall at intervals, with several routes set alongside each one. The rope is connected to the wall itself by an anchor point. Whilst there are a few variations, generally they involve a solid ring of metal hanging off two equally solid chains which are themselves bolted onto the wall by some equally solid bolts… SOLID!

The climber attaches themselves to one end of rope, the belayer to another and, "HEY PRESTO!" off they go... Well theoretically "yes", but as much as it is important that the rope is attached to the wall/rock, it is equally important that the climber and belayer are attached CORRECTLY to the rope. Let's start with the person you're probably most interested in right now:

The climber and the rope - a love story

How a climber safely attaches to a rope

To safely attach YOU, the climber, to a rope you will need an additional piece of kit: a climbing harness. Now, lucky for you, I have included a section on harnesses in the next chapter, handily entitled (yes, you've guessed it) 'Harnesses'.

Whilst I too wouldn't find reading a section of a book called 'Harnesses' very appealing, the harness plays a key part in keeping you safe – there's not a lot of point in having one if you haven't put it on correctly or its faulty - so investing 10 minutes of reading time for your continued safety and wellbeing is ~~probably~~ DEFINITELY worth it!

Readers who failed to look at the 'Harnesses' section

Whilst there are a bazillion different types of climbing harness, there is one universally approved means of connecting the rope to the harness, and that requires the ability to tie a knot. And KNOT JUST ANY NOT… I mean… NOT JUST ANY KNOT! (Not only will this next piece of information potentially save your life, but it could also be mildly useful in a quiz setting where, for example, the question is, "What knot is commonly used by climbers to attach themselves to the rope?" Here's hoping, eh?!). It is of course, a RETHREADED FIGURE OF EIGHT KNOT.

Now I can barely tie my shoelaces, but I can happily tie a figure of eight knot (Thinking about it, maybe I should tie my shoelaces WITH a figure of eight knot). It becomes simple once you've practised it a few times. Although the description below may require 'a willing suspension of disbelief', it is commonly used by instructors to help students visualise the knot tying process.

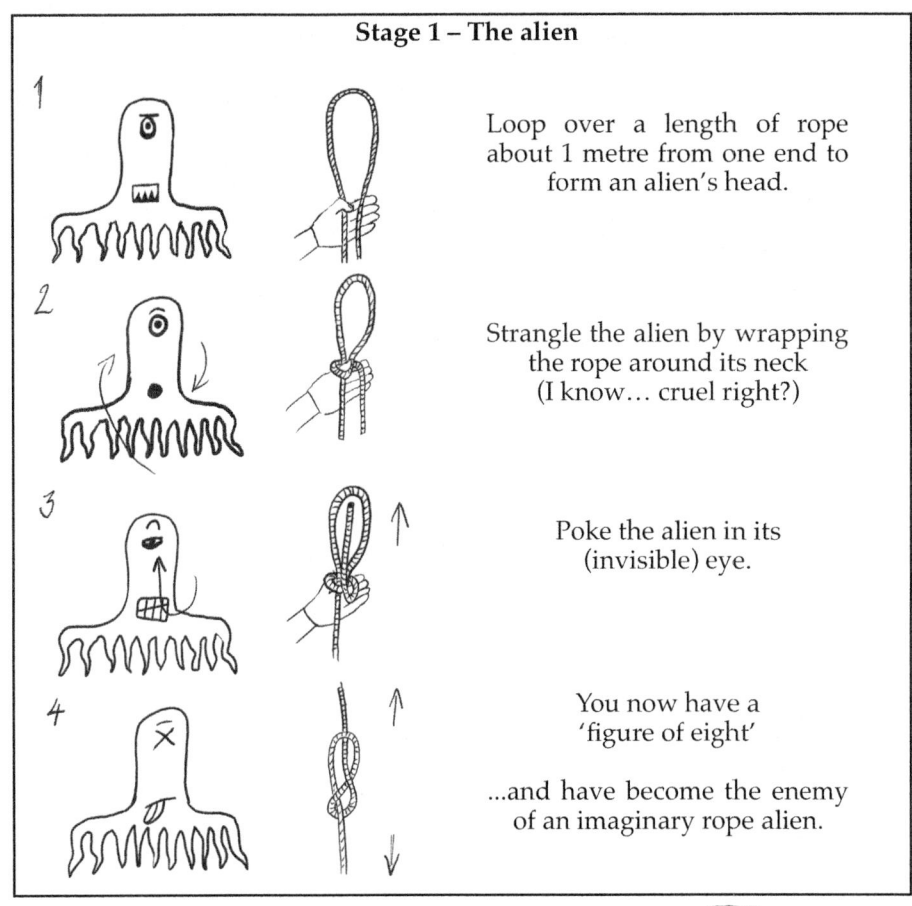

Stage 1 – The alien

1 Loop over a length of rope about 1 metre from one end to form an alien's head.

2 Strangle the alien by wrapping the rope around its neck (I know... cruel right?)

3 Poke the alien in its (invisible) eye.

4 You now have a 'figure of eight'

...and have become the enemy of an imaginary rope alien.

Stage 2 - Thread the ~~needle~~ rope

You must now thread the rope through the two specific tying in points on your harness, normally consisting of one loop attached to the waist belt and one loop attached to the leg loops.

Make sure you don't confuse the tie-in loops with your belay loop.

...I told you you needed to read the section on harnesses!

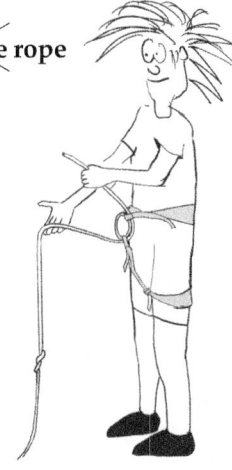

Stage 3 – Racing cars

Align the end of the rope with the existing figure of eight and get your loose piece of rope to follow the same route, like a racing car driving along the track... (Yeah, okay, I get that this requires come serious imagination, but it will help... HONEST!)

You should have a fist sized figure of eight knot with a length of rope forming a 'tail', ideally no more than 30cm long.

Stage 4 - The stopper knot

You can put your imagination on hold here... this is just another knot... But still good for those pesky quiz questions...

Grab the spare tail and wrap it twice around the main length of rope so that it is just in front of the rethreaded figure of eight knot. Then tuck the short remaining rope back underneath itself, pulling tight. You may find it helpful to use your thumb as a guide... but remember to remove it once you have finished the knot!

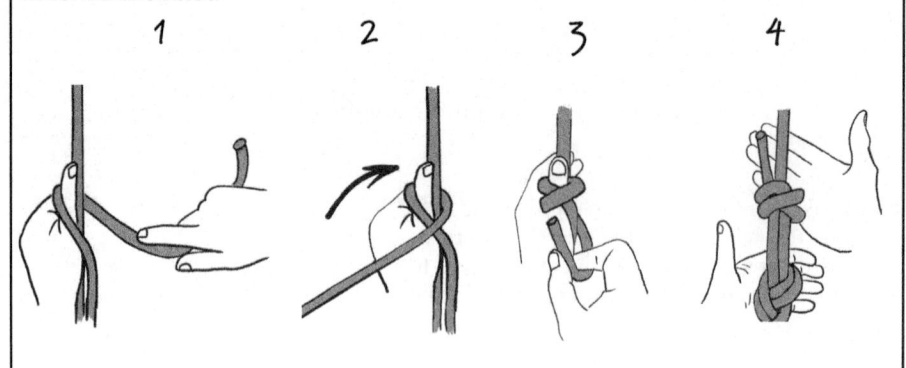

1   2   3   4

The fact that you can tie a stopper knot shows you've got enough tail to stop your lovingly constructed figure of eight knot from unravelling. It's also a handy means of keeping the loose end of the rope from getting in the way.

Stage 5 - Mission control pre-launch checks

You've tied your figure of eight and stopper knots. Stage 5 is simple. Now YOU need to give it a thorough inspection. Then, get your CLIMBING PARTNER to also check that the rope is secured to your harness correctly and that your knots are tied appropriately. You can return the favour and check that they tie into their belay device safely.

This BUDDY CHECK system is an important habit to get into, providing the two essential people in this climbing venture an extra level of security. And, if either of you are in any doubt – ask a COMPETENT CLIMBER/CLIMBING INSTRUCTOR to check it all for you.

The belayer and the rope - a love affair

How a belayer safely attaches to the rope

"You will need...

1 x reliable, grounded, alcohol and drug-free, friend or associate who has had proper training from a qualified instructor

1 x well-fitting climbing harness

1 x belay device

1 locking karabiner..."

So, if you're anything like me with a recipe book in the kitchen, you'll only have half the ingredients and a few items you won't even have heard of! As a belayer, all the listed 'ingredients' are essential, otherwise, metaphorically speaking, your cake won't rise. Let's go through each to be sure:

- **1 x reliable, grounded, alcohol and drug-free, friend or associate who has had proper training from a qualified instructor**

Let me stress again – to safely rope climb you need a COMPETENT BELAYER, because your life - you know, the only one you get - may depend on it.

Scenario A

You are a heartless, rude, and widely disliked octogenarian billionaire. Your young, promiscuous wife, who has recently changed the details of your will so that your entire fortune will go to her in the event of a climbing accident, says she will belay you.

...THINK AGAIN!

Scenario B

You are a keen and enthusiastic young climber who is enthralled by the idea of rope climbing for the first time and, eager to learn, watches a few YouTube videos before, "giving it a go with a mate".

...THINK AGAIN!

Scenario C

You get some proper training from a qualified instructor and survive to tell the tale.

...RIGHT DECISION EINSTEIN!

It's actually very difficult to determine if someone is a competent belayer if you haven't had any training yourself (you won't necessarily pick up on whether they're doing it right or wrong).

Fortunately, most climbing gyms insist that the climber demonstrates how to tie in, and the belayer demonstrates how to belay (and vice versa), before they are allowed to use the rope climbing area. After all, a climbing gym littered with the bodies of poorly belayed climbers wouldn't be a great business model.

"They looked like they might know what they were doing..."

It pays to find someone who might be interested in an 'introduction to rope climbing course' so that you get to 'learn the ropes' at the same time. You will soon know whether you want them belaying you (or NOT!).

As it happens, sometimes the best and safest belayers are those who have only just started. This is because they are not entirely comfortable with the process and so check and recheck everything they do. A good mentality to retain!

- **1 x well-fitting climbing harness**

See 'The Climber and the rope' section and when you've read that… read Chapter 10 which covers choosing the correct harness.

- **1 x belay device**

Whilst in days of old, belayers used to control the rope by wrapping it around their waist (although still practiced by some traditional types), us MODERN FOLK tend to use a belay device. Belay devices act as a FRICTION BRAKE. This means you don't have to rely on brute strength and a prayer to stop a climber from hitting the dirt. Whilst there are many on the market, the most common are tubular belay devices made from aluminium. They are relatively cheap to purchase and straight forward to use.

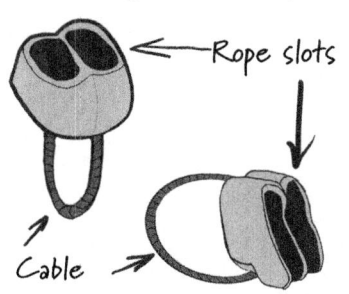

Essentially the rope runs freely through the device, unless the belayer wants to stop it, such as in the instance of a climber falling. At this point, the belayer pulls the rope in a direction that applies MAXIMUM FRICTION against the belay device, thereby arresting any further descent.

- **1 x locking Karabiner (aka Carabiner, Krab, Crab or Biner)**

Karabiners have a wide variety of uses in climbing, but for the purposes of belaying, the karabiner is to connect the rope, via the belay device, to the belayer's harness. The karabiner is effectively the attachment securing the belayer to the rope, so it is essential that you use a karabiner certified for this purpose.

The 'D' shaped karabiner lends itself to belaying because the rope naturally tends to pull it lengthways (on its MAJOR AXIS – the strongest axis) when 'loaded' under tension. And don't worry, there aren't A, B, C, E, F, etc shaped karabiners to choose from – D is standard!

A karabiner is strongest when the 'gate' is closed. An open karabiner isn't just weaker when loaded, it is downright dangerous. My dad once shouted at me, "There's no point in having a gate if you don't ****** well shut it!" He wasn't talking about a karabiner at the time (the dog had just escaped out of the garden and run off down the road!), but the sentiment is the same.

It is highly advisable to obtain a LOCKING karabiner, that is one where the

Open gate

gate automatically 'clicks shut' (the aptly named AUTO-LOCKING karabiner) or is manually screwed shut (the equally aptly named SCREWGATE karabiner). Whilst auto-locking karabiners are hassle-free, it's always important to check that the gate has clicked shut and not just 'clicked'! In comparison, a screwgate karabiner allows you to screw the gate shut so you can be assured it's closed. But always remember, "RIGHTY TIGHTY, LEFTY LOOSEY"... I can't count the number of times I tried to undo the gate and accidentally tightened it up instead.

Mixing your ingredients (Setting up to belay)

- A karabiner should be attached to the belay loop of the belayer's harness.

- The belayer must slide a U-shaped length of rope (a bight) through the rope slots of the belay device. There are usually two slots. I tend to use the one nearest my dominant hand.

- The karabiner (attached to the belayer's harness) should be attached to both (1) the rope and (2) the belay device cable.

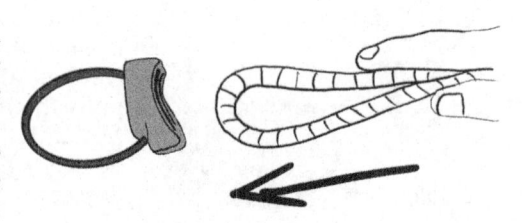

Rope
Belay device cable

- The karabiner should be in the closed/locked position.

If you made a cake missing a key ingredient, its likely to be a complete catastrophe. As a belayer, you're not making a cake, you're keeping someone alive! So, before you even consider belaying, check everything, and then get the climber to recheck your set up too.

1, 2, 3 and 1, 2, 3 and brake

Belay technique as the climber ascends the wall

With top rope belaying there is a specific sequence to follow which may, at least at first, seem as confusing as patting your head and rubbing your stomach at the same time. With practice however, belaying becomes automatic. And with the right instruction, you will belay efficiently and safely. But it is essential that you learn correctly from the start. Reading about it will not be sufficient and could lead to **injury** or **death**. Not a nice thought. I can't think of a more subtle hint though… Just… NO! NO!

To supplement your understanding of the process:

- As the climber ascends the wall, the belayer must TAKE IN rope by pulling the rope towards the belay device with one hand, and pulling excess rope through the belay device with the other.

- LIVE ROPE goes from the belay device to the climber. DEAD ROPE goes from the belay device to the floor.

- The belayer pulls the dead rope through the belay device as the climber ascends.

- A belayer must always have one hand firmly gripping the dead rope so that they can control the amount of rope that passes through the belay device.

- Pay special attention here: The hand on the dead rope is called the BRAKE HAND. … if you can't brake, you can't stop the rope, and if you can't stop the rope, you can't stop the climber if they fall, and if you can't stop the climber if they fall then you are of no use whatsoever.

- It's best to have the brake hand placed a few inches below the belay device so that there is no chance of your hand or fingers getting caught in arrangement.

- The belayer's other hand holds the live rope, pulling excess rope towards the belay device.

- The belayer will temporarily let go of the live rope to aid pulling excess slack through the belay device, before replacing it.

- The sequence is oft simplified as, "V to the knee, 1, 2, 3"

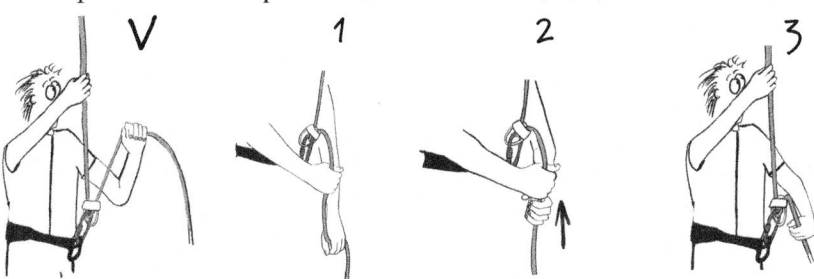

As a climber ascends, the rope needs to be pulled through the belay device, so that there is virtually little or no slack in the rope (Remember – the more slack, the further the climber is going to fall). Continue sequence until the climber:

(a)　finishes climbing or
(b)　falls.

Either way, the belayer is going to need to apply the brake. This simply involves pulling the brake hand down (for most devices) and 'locking off', a reassuringly simple, yet amazingly effective means of stopping any further progress of the rope and therefore the climber.

Lowering

Once a climber has reached the top of a climb (i.e. to the anchor suspending the rope) or as far as they want to/can climb, they're going to want to come back down (I know, after all that effort… it's a bizarre sport!). Like everything in climbing, it's perfectly safe if it's done properly. So, here's a demonstration sequence of events:

Climber reaches the anchor, "WHOOPS!" with the sense of achievement, and then looks down to the belayer to check they are aware that the climb is complete. The belayer takes in any remaining slack and, with BOTH HANDS ON THE DEADROPE, takes the climbers weight.

As it happens, a lot of climbers can get nervy of this next stage: The climber lets go of any holds and, holding onto the rope, slowly leans back away from the wall. It can be a VERY WEIRD feeling. After all that time desperately holding on to each hold for dear life, you must simply let go… and lean out into thin air!

The belayer lowers, with one hand maintaining the brake and the other smoothly feeding the rope through the belay device. The climber essentially walks backwards down the wall.

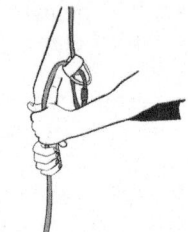

Climbers

DON'T jump backwards and forwards off the wall as you descend… you are not a member of an elite military special forces unit (although I suppose you can do this if you ARE a member of an elite military special forces unit!), because there's a chance you'll miss your footing, come off balance, and flip into the wall; or simply irritate your belayer (Avoid irritating someone in charge of your LIFE)!

Belayers

DON'T run the rope through the belay device super quick to scare your climber… no one wants a superfast descent, even, "for a laugh". A simple mistiming could result in serious injury, and then nobody's gonna be laughing!

Weight differential

Have you ever seen a picture of one of the giant catapults, used by the Roman military artillery, to sling enormous boulders into the walls of a besieged town under attack? (Okay, just because I said "boulders", stop thinking about climbing for one second). Well, now imagine standing in the trough where they normally put the boulders ready for firing…. Now imagine what it would be like if a Roman General decided to fire YOU at the besieged town… One second you're standing still, the next you've been launched into the air at a colossal speed…

Well, that's exactly the feeling I had when a friend, twice my weight, fell off the top of the wall while I was belaying him. One second I was standing still, the next – "WHOOOOOOOSH!" - I had launched into the air, flying a metre up the wall before coming to an abrupt stop almost level with him. At that moment, I asked myself three questions:

Question 1

What THE HELL just happened?

Question 2

How am I going to get back down?

Question 3

Do I have a change of underpants?!!!!

The answers were surprisingly simple…

Answer 1

There was a lot of slack in the system so that when he fell, he fell further than was necessary (I should have had him on tight reins). The further he fell, the more energy he generated and this, combined with the weight difference between us, meant that I was pulled up the wall.

Answer 2

Fortunately I had kept my brake hand firmly down and in place, so as soon as our weights equalised – like on a set of scales – neither of us were going anywhere. On this occasion, he regained his composure, clambered back onto some holds and I slowly and carefully fed the rope through the belay device, lowering myself down the wall, followed by him.

Answer 3

No - Why would I have brought a spare pair of underpants to a climbing wall?! Although it might be worth packing some, at least when you first start out!

In an ideal world, climbing partners would be roughly the same weight. But even when they are the same weight, should the climber fall from a great height with slack 'in the system', they're still going to generate enough energy to at least give the belayer a jolt.

In the same way that a climber shouldn't be afraid of falling, a belayer shouldn't be afraid of CATCHING and HOLDING a falling climber. With any fall, the dynamic rope will stretch and the knots (you have perfectly tied!) will tighten, both of which will help absorb some of the energy generated.

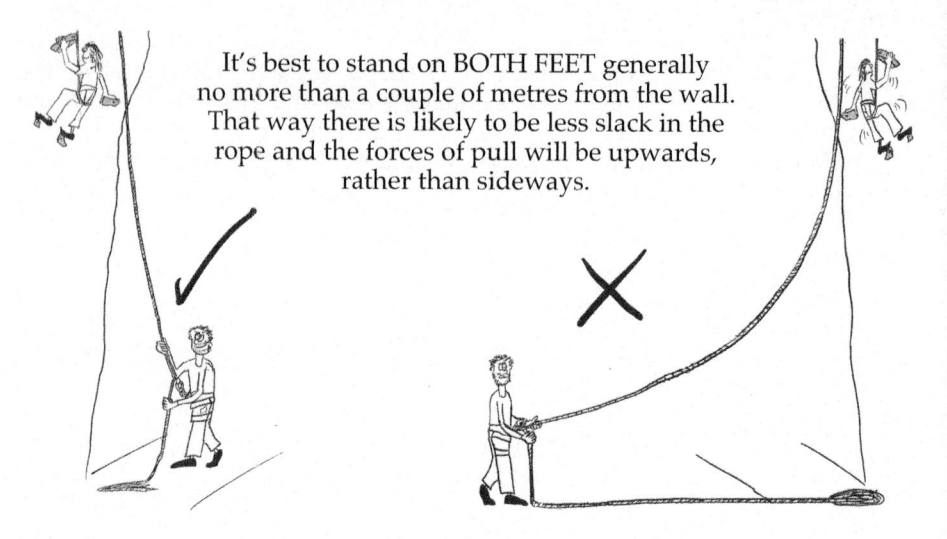

It's best to stand on BOTH FEET generally no more than a couple of metres from the wall. That way there is likely to be less slack in the rope and the forces of pull will be upwards, rather than sideways.

For climbing partners who are vastly difference weights, it needn't necessarily be a problem. Imagine you are a giant hot air balloon… you don't want to float off into the sunset, you want to stay in one spot and do a bit of belaying. To ensure your feet don't have a chance of leaving the ground, you can tie yourself onto a specially designed WEIGHT BAG (essentially a bag that is heavy) or GROUND ANCHOR, either of which is likely to be available at your chosen climbing gym. This means that even if your climbing partner is heavy… you're NOT GOING ANYWHERE!

CLIMBERS - Check, check and check again.

So, all your life you've been used to being close to the ground, your feet on the floor. When you climb, your feet – and the rest of you - are going to be a long way off the ground. Naturally this may make you feel a little anxious. A little bit of anxiety is a good thing. The adrenaline in your body keeps you alert and responsive. But it's also a time when you don't want unhelpful thoughts creeping into your mind. There are innumerable occasions when I have climbed high above my own comfort zone, when I suddenly think, "Did I tie-in properly?" I think you'll agree – the last place on earth you want to be worrying whether you are safely tied onto a rope is when you're hanging so far off the ground people look like ants!

If you have checked your set up, then you will settle any unconscious worries that might suddenly surface when you're halfway up the wall. And when I say check, I mean CHECK... not just a cursory glance. Have you threaded the rope through the correct (tie-in) loops? Have you tied a bona fide rethreaded figure of eight and stopper knot? Have you made sure there are no straps, pieces of clothing or other items (e.g. unnecessary jewellery, long hair, pet python, etc) that might get in the way once climbing commences?

As previously mentioned, get into the habit of doing a BUDDY CHECK. Get your buddy, the belayer, to check your set up. And then, in turn check that their karabiner is locked and securely fastened to the correct part of their harness, and that the rope and belay device is attached properly and functioning normally. That way you should both have the utmost confidence that all the equipment is match fit for the task before you start your ascent.

BELAYERS - Clear the ground around you!

When safely belaying, you will be looking up at the climber on the wall and not at your feet. So, if you've left anything on the floor, you'll probably trip over it. Place bags, stinky or pristine climbing shoes, your packed lunch, and any other potential trip hazards far out of the way. You don't want to be falling over whilst belaying, because the first thing you'll want to do when falling is... put your hands out (After all, no one wants to break a fall with their face!). Have you guessed the problem with this yet? Of course, you have... CATASTROPHE!

Picture it:

Your buddy is 40 feet up the wall, just going for the highest and most difficult crimp. Staring up in awe, you step forward to get a better view, but your foot lands on a water bottle which rolls, sending you off balance. Instinctively, you put your hands out, but in doing so, release the rope at the very moment your climbing partner has missed a hold. As you land on your front uninjured, your climbing partner hits the ground next to you... and they don't look very well!

BELAYERS - Concentrate on what you're doing!

My wife complains that none of the jobs in the house ever get done because I can't multitask. "PAH! RUBBISH!" I shout at her, whilst running away (at the same time demonstrating my incredible multitasking ability – talking, running, and avoiding whatever job she had for me). But I must grudgingly admit she is right: I am much better at doing one task at a time. That is why, if I find myself belaying, I JUST BELAY. I don't chat to passers-by, read texts on my phone, or even look around.

Remember what I said about climbers generally being very sociable? It's not uncommon for someone to spark up a conversation while you are belaying. After all, they can't chat to a climber who is halfway up the wall. As polite individuals, many of us might find it difficult NOT to engage. No one wants to be rude. But think: are you really concentrating on what you are doing? How is your climbing partner going to feel if they turn and see you gassing? So, have a few stock phrases at the ready: "I'll be with you when they're safely back on the ground!", "I'll be with you in a minute!", or my personal favourite, "If you don't want to be responsible for the serious injury or death of my climbing partner, then please stop talking to me you despicable fiend!" There is only one person you need to be communicating with... the climber... After all, their life is literally in your hands!

A good belayer will watch the climber's ascent, pre-empting when they might need more slack to manoeuvre, or less (i.e. a tighter rope) such as when, for example, attempting a difficult section. When the rope is slack, a climber can barely feel its presence and may almost forget it is there. Conversely, in a difficult or challenging section, a tighter rope (i.e. less slack) can help a climber feel reassuringly secure. In fact, the most vulnerable time for a climber on a top rope climb is right at the start when they are close to the ground. So, although if a climber did fall, they wouldn't fall very far, if they're not that far off the ground to begin with, they could hit the deck and potentially twist their ankle, jolt their knees, or worse. So... it pays to have a super tight rope at the start. Other than that, the risks associated with falling on a top rope are extremely low.

Watching the climber from afar enables the belayer to provide advice if the climber needs help. For example, the location of a good hold may be more obvious to the belayer who is in a position to survey the whole route, rather than to the climber who is up close to the wall.

Also, if a belayer is watching intently, they will be much more likely to react in the SPLIT-SECOND it takes for a climber to suddenly fall.

"There's literally nothing to hold on to!"

BEST HOLD IN THE COUNTRY

A good belayer might already anticipate where a fall is likely – such as the trickiest section of a climb – and know to be on HIGH ALERT for a potential fall.

CLIMBERS - Understand what you are climbing!

In the same way that you should choose boulder routes that are within your range of ability, aim to tackle those rope climbs you have at least a chance of completing. Roquefort, the metric system, Bridgit Bardot, and champagne - zee French have given us many things including the FRENCH SPORT GRADE SYSTEM, a sliding scale of difficulty that is used in most climbing centres in Europe (N.B. This is not to be confused with the, similarly French, but bouldering specific 'Fontainebleau' grade system (See the appendices for useful conversion charts of the most commonly used bouldering and sport climbing grade systems in Europe and the USA).

Grades start at 1 (which is basically about as difficult as getting up the set of steps you walked up to get into the climbing gym) through to 9c with the numbers, letters, and pluses (+) identifying intermediate steps between the grades:

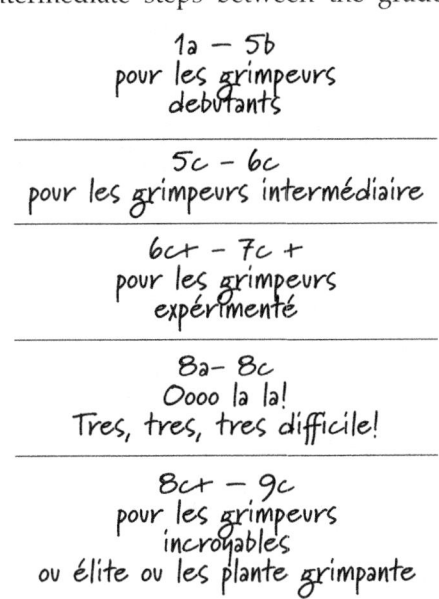

"Zis starts off – how you say – Easy-peasy..."

1a – 5b
pour les grimpeurs debutants

5c – 6c
pour les grimpeurs intermédiaire

6c+ – 7c +
pour les grimpeurs expérimenté

"...but becomes impossible!"

8a– 8c
Oooo la la!
Tres, tres, tres difficile!

8c+ – 9c
pour les grimpeurs incroyables
ou élite ou les plante grimpante

COM-MUUUUUN-IC-AAAA-TION

Stand 15 metres apart from your friend across a crowded climbing gym and get them to shout instructions to you. I guarantee you won't be able to understand everything that is being said. When climbing, rather than being horizontal, one of you will be going VERTICAL...

When you're dangling on the end of a rope, or as a belayer, in charge of someone dangling on the end of the rope, there is never a more important time to communicate in a quick and concise manner.

"I just want you to pull in a little rope because I think I may slip in a sec... but I've got enough loose rope at the moment..."

"Could you just say the first bit again..."

Even when climbing outdoors in apparent isolation, the sound of the wind, a bird call, or a plane flying overhead can break the silence… and your concentration, which is why a few recognised climbing terms are worth remembering! Universally used, here are a few key terms that help rule out any confusion:

"CLIMB WHEN READY" – The belayer is essentially saying, "I'm ready when you are…"

"CLIMBING" – The climber is ready and starts the route…Yeah, I know… Obvs…! But listen here: there are countless occasions when I have seen a climber start up a route and the belayer hasn't even noticed. You're only safe when your belayer is actually belaying!

Saying "CLIMBING" gives the belayer notice that you're effectively off the starting blocks and on the wall. They can then get the rope pulled in promptly as you ascend, ensuring that, even if you slip from a low height, they have their hand ready on the brake so there's no risk of you hitting the ground.

"Yeah, so I was telling you about my holiday. Well, on the first day…"

"TAKE" or **"TAKE IN"** – The climber is asking the belayer to take in (i.e. tighten up) any loose rope and lock off (i.e. brake position). It's a term often used when the climber might be feeling a bit nervous of a move and want (a) the belayer to be prepared and (b) to limit the distance of the fall (i.e. you won't fall as far when there is tension in the rope).

Not to be confused with "SNAKE!" in the event you have just disturbed a deadly king cobra. To avoid confusion in this unlikely event, I would consider using an alternative phrase such as, "HOLY FLIP, A GIANT POISONOUS REPTILIAN INVERTEBRATE!"

"SLACK" - Don't be offended if the climber shouts this at you – they're not having a go at your relaxed attitude - it simply means, "GIVE ME EXTRA ROPE!". The climber may just feel the rope is too tight and/or restricting their ability to make a move. However, if someone is shouting "SLACK" at you anywhere other than a climbing wall you may want to clarify what they mean!

"FALLING" – There will come a point in every climber's life where they know they can't hang on any longer - a fall is inevitable - and that's the moment to yell, in the most calm and collective manner you can muster, "FALLING!" It acts as a MISSILE WARNING SYSTEM ALARM for the belayer, snapping them into readiness to catch the fall.

"WATCH ME" - On the approach to a difficult sequence of moves, if your climbing colleague suddenly shouts "WATCH ME!" don't mistake it as a vain boast…

Regard "WATCH ME" as the prequel to "FALLING". It could signify the climber is anxious about the next move or moves and so wants reassurance that their belayer is going to be ready.

"WATCH ME" = "Be prepared". And, of course, a good belayer will be watching the whole time anyway!

Automatic belay

Many climbing gyms will have fixed auto-belay devices which allow people to climb at height without the need for a belayer. They're great for practicing longer, vertical routes, and especially good it you don't have any mates!

A few years ago, I decided to invest in a new hosepipe. I know, 'rock n roll' heh?! My old one was always coiled in a heap in the garden and, consequently, I regularly tripped over it. So, I bought a new hosepipe reel encased in a plastic cover. Whenever I need the hosepipe, I just pull, and metres and metres of hose come out, like hankies from a magician's sleeve. However, the *pièce de résistance* is that, when I've finished with it, I just let go of the end and the whole hosepipe is sucked back into the casing. Auto-belays look a little bit like an enclosed hosepipe reel hanging off the ceiling. They consist of a reel of webbing which is retractable, coiled up inside the plastic cover (like my hosepipe) and extremely strong (unlike my hosepipe). I know what you're thinking, "But can it squirt water?" (The auto-belay, not the hose pipe... of course the hosepipe can squirt water). No, sadly I have never heard of an auto-belay that squirts water. But, after ascending a route, it will safely lower you back down to the ground (which is more than my hosepipe reel would do). Thankfully, they are very straight forward to use, but there are some basic things to remember to avoid accident, injury, or just looking like a doofus...

The auto-belay will usually have a locking karabiner on the end which will be clipped onto a retainer on the floor or wall. It's clipped in because the auto-belay device works on tension, so when you unclip, don't let go, which is what I did on my first use, as the auto-belay will automatically retract and pull the karabiner up to the top of the route without a climber on the end...

And unless you have brought a pair of your own stilts, you're going to have to go 'cap in hand' to the gym staff and ask them to retrieve it, or skulk away hoping no one has seen you (everyone would have seen you)!

So, if you're going to use the auto-belay, make sure that you keep hold of it once you've unclipped it from the retainer. Clip the karabiner onto your belay loop (remember that's the thick band of material at the front of your harness).

Auto-belay karabiners tend to be auto-locking, requiring a push-and-twist to open, which then snaps shut once you let go. The main thing to be sure of is that the gate is completely shut. If you're not sure, ASK someone to check. It's good practice to give the auto-belay webbing a tug before you set off to check that it is retracting smoothly.

Once you're clipped in, you're ready to climb. It's literally that simple. It's so simple in fact that some people have been known to start climbing without clipping in at all! Remember, unlike top roping, there is no belayer and therefore no one to buddy check you, SO MAKE SURE YOU SELF-CHECK YOU ARE CLIPPED IN BEFORE YOU START!!!!!!

Good climbing gyms tend to have signage at the start of the route saying, "MAKE SURE YOU'RE CLIPPED IN". If you are clipped in, you can obviously just ignore them. If, during your climb, you suddenly realise you're not clipped in (believe me, it can happen very easily), then take a deep breath, carefully climb back down, and kiss the ground because that could've been a very messy end to the day.

Good time to check if you're clipped in correctly

Really bad time to check you're clipped in correctly

Assuming you are clipped in correctly, then you can climb up the route to your heart's content, safe in the knowledge that if you fall, this automatic system will catch you. Doesn't mean it's not going to feel a bit weird the first few times. You do see a lot of people tentatively climbing back down rather than letting go at all. If you think you might have TRUST ISSUES, then fall/jump off after a short distance and be reassured that the auto-belay device is going to slowly lower you to the ground.

Some additional safety measures to consider:

- Try not to bash your head on the auto-belay device at the top of a climb and never climb beyond it!

- Make sure you just climb the route directly beneath the auto-belay. If you move sideways to something that looks a bit more interesting, the result is that you're likely to swing if you fall, which sounds fun, until you go careering into another climber or the wall! Either way you'll be about as popular with the climbing gym staff as a wrecking ball in a greenhouse.

- Finally, before you let go at the top of the climb, it's worth checking below, just in case someone is standing in your landing zone. Although most climbing gyms tend to mark the area, it's surprising how many people still inadvertently wander into the zone. Landing on a person - even a large, squishy person - is NOT going to be a comfortable landing, so if there is anyone there call out, "LOOK OUT BELOW!", "DUUUUUUDE! I'M ABOUT TO LAND ON YOUR HEAD!" or something more explicit!

The least you need to know

- In top rope climbing, the rope runs through a fixed point on the wall called an anchor.

- A climber must attach themselves to one end of the rope, fed through the tying in points on their harness, and secured by a rethreaded figure of eight and stopper knot.

- A belayer attaches a belay device to their harness using a locking or screwgate karabiner. The belay device enables the belayer to use friction as a means of controlling the rope.

- A climber and belayer should always do a BUDDY CHECK before each climb, ensuring that their equipment is properly fitted and in good working order.

- When belaying, make sure the ground is clear around you, do not get distracted by others, concentrate on how the climber is progressing - whether they need more (feed out slack) or less (feed in slack) rope - and be prepared to catch a fall. Never let go of the dead rope.

- Climbing routes are commonly graded using the French Sport Grade system, ranging from 1 to 9c+.

- To aid communication, climbers and belayers should familiarise themselves with some short terms, including: "READY TO CLIMB", "CLIMBING", "TAKE (IN)", "SLACK", "WATCH ME", and "FALLING".

- An auto-belay is a device that enables people to climb high walls without the need for a belayer. It is essential that you check you are clipped in BEFORE you start climbing.

10
EQUIPPED FOR SUCCESS: MORE ESSENTIAL KIT

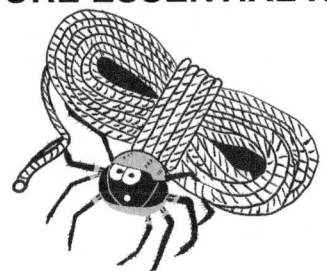

If you're getting into rope climbing, then there are some additional pieces of equipment that are worth investing in. This chapter provides a basic guide to purchasing the right:

- Helmet.
- Harness.
- Rope.

1. Climbing Helmets

Search the internet and watch some videos of the world's best climbers and you'll see a lot of them scaling cliffs without a helmet. The reasons for this are no doubt plentiful:

- It messes with my hair...
- It gets in the way...
- My sponsors want me to be clearly identifiable...
- My head is the size of a beachball...
- I look cool WITHOUT the helmet...

Wearing a helmet is a matter of choice, but you must weigh up the risk of NOT wearing one against the likelihood of injury.

The purpose of a climbing helmet is to protect your head against anything that could injure you whilst climbing. Outdoors, rockfall is perhaps the most obvious example. An individual rope climbing up a cliff face could potentially dislodge loose rocks onto themselves or, perhaps worse still, the belayer below (Consider the consequences for a climber if their belayer gets knocked out by a falling rock!). Wearing a helmet makes absolute sense.

"He was a totally awesome climber... well, until a rock fell on his head!"

Of course, indoor climbing gyms don't generally suffer from rockfalls! There may well be a chance of someone's sweets falling out of their pocket and landing on your bonce, but other than getting a sherbet lemon in your ear, you shouldn't have to worry about anything falling onto your head.

As bouldering, indoors and outdoors, tends to be comparatively close to the ground, less climbers choose to climb with a helmet.

In fact, many indoor climbing gyms discourage helmets for bouldering because of the small, but nonetheless possible, risk of getting a helmet strap caught on a climbing hold.

Whether you are climbing indoors or outdoors, be alive to the fact that there is always a chance of banging your head on the route up - particularly if you haven't judged the position of a jutting out hold or an overhang – or hitting you head on the way down (e.g. a bad fall). For rope climbing, probably the biggest single risk is when a climber slips from a hold and swings into the wall. In the worst-case scenario, where you hit the wall backwards using your head as a brake, the importance of an impact absorbing helmet is clear!

Choosing a helmet

Okay... you've got a bicycle helmet and you want to save some cash. So, just wear it climbing; right?

WRONG!!!

Helmets are designed to provide protection against risks specific to different sporting activities. So, a bike helmet is unlikely to have the overhead protection that a climbing specific helmet would have.

"Safety comes first!"

The first thing you need to do is ensure that any helmet you purchase meets the industry standard for rock climbing. Ask! Any reputable outdoor or sporting goods store should be able to provide advice. If your helmet description doesn't indicate it is suitable protection for rock climbing... assume it isn't!

There are two basic types of helmet: HARD SHELL and SOFT SHELL. Initially it sounds obvious which one you'd want... I mean what possible use is a soft shell?!!!! Don't get too many squashy backed tortoises, do you? Just hear me out:

Hard shell helmets are just that… the inside is foam lined for comfort and the outside is… well… hard. They are generally made from polycarbonate (hard plastic to you and me) and tend to be durable and affordable.

Soft shell helmets are usually made of foam…

"That's my soft shell sorted for this afternoon's climb!"

Actually, high quality expanded polystyrene covered in a thin plastic layer. As you'd expect, they're very light and comfortable to wear. What you might not realise is that they are also rather good at impact protection. They'd have to be really, otherwise there wouldn't be much of a market for them!

Choosing a helmet, whether it be hard shell, soft shell, or a combination of the two (hybrid) - should be based on a number of variables, including:

- Cost (soft shell and hybrid can be a lot more expensive).
- Weather (e.g. does it have vents to let the heat escape).
- Location of intended climbing (e.g. brightly coloured in the mountains - be safe be seen!).
- Type of climbing (e.g. lighter helmet for extended climbs).

But, most importantly, it has to FIT CORRECTLY!

Unlike climbing shoes, a snug fit isn't necessarily a good thing. A helmet that is too tight can cause a headache, which isn't exactly going to encourage you to keep wearing it. It should, however, be secure enough that, if you shake your head, it doesn't just fly off!

There's no harm in trying on a few different helmets to find the best match.

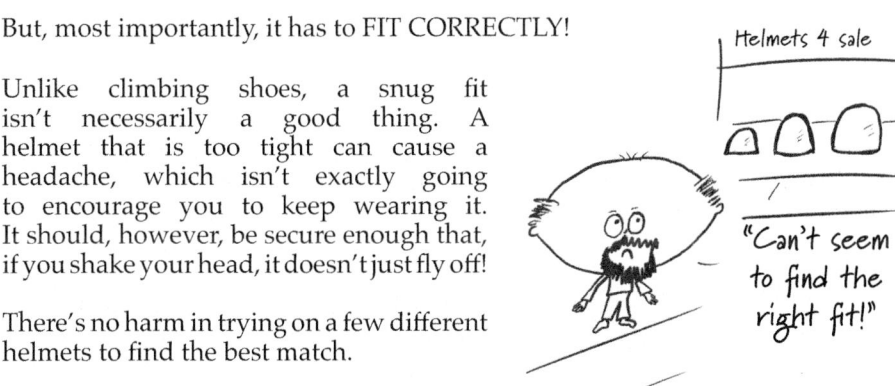

Helmets 4 sale

"Can't seem to find the right fit!"

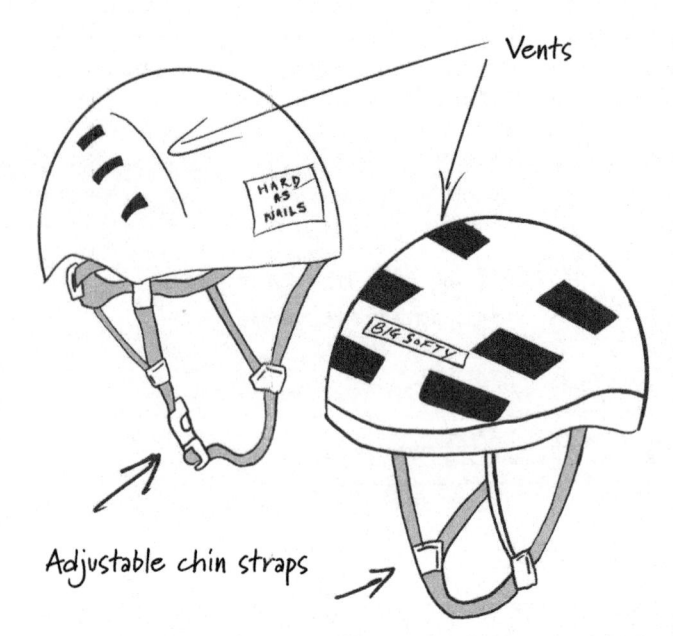

A good way of testing the fit is to place the helmet on your head (obvs!) and then nod, tilt your head back, and then shake side to side. If there's not much slippage, then things are looking promising.

Climbing helmets are fitted with straps which should be fastened firmly under the chin. Too loose and the helmet risks falling off, too tight and you risk garrotting yourself!

Sooooooo, imagine you've just bought your brand spanking new helmet but, as you exit the store, your helmet leaps out of the shopping bag like it's got a life of its own and rolls down the pavement, clattering to a stop. If you picked it up and discovered it was dented or cracked, then feel free to shout numerous profanities at the top of your voice, because you're going to have to get a new one.

"No way!" you say, "I've paid too much money – it'll be fine!"

Ladies and gentlemen let me present my case: Firstly, I require a willing volunteer… (Yeah – that's you).

For the purpose of this demonstration I also require a raw egg (Humour me; get an egg out of the fridge… or out of a chicken… whichever is closer).

Now, hold the egg between thumb and forefinger along its LONG AXIS….

Squeeze your finger and thumb together as hard as you can….

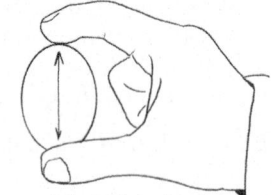

If my experiment worked, you should find that you couldn't break the egg. Chicken eggs have a compressive strength of 100lbs, meaning you need to apply considerable force before it will break. If you want to go completely crazy, add a bottle top to the bottom and top of the egg and balance a book on top of it… make a book mountain if you wish… the strength is incredible.

However, put a tiny crack or dent in that egg and try the experiment again (Actually, do it outside!). If my calculations are correct, the egg is likely to have shattered…

The point is, damage to an egg considerably weakens its structural strength and, in the same way, damage to a climbing helmet means it is unlikely to afford the protection it would have done.

So don't risk having egg on your face: If you damage your helmet, suck it up and buy a new one!

EGGSELLENT choice...

2. Harness the knowledge (Harnesses!)

The harness is another integral piece of kit for rope climbing because it is what connects you with the rope... and there's little point having a rope at all if you're not connected. Most indoor climbing gyms hire out harnesses, but if you're going to climb regularly it's worth investing in one that you're confident wearing and is a comfortable fit.

A harness consists of:

- A waist belt which wraps around your waist like a normal belt except that it's secured by one or two buckles.

- Leg loops that you step into, which sit around your thighs. Often, they are adjustable and, if you're lucky, padded for extra comfort. Some harnesses include elastic straps which can alter the distance between the waist belt and leg loops.

- A belay loop is the only place on the harness you should attach your karabiner and belay device when belaying or an auto-belay karabiner. Made of nylon webbing, the belay loop is super strong and will have been subject to 'load testing' – like an extreme strength test - before being certified as usable.

- Tie-in loops are also known as tie-in points or tie-in holes, and a climber's rope should go through both upper and lower ones to ensure that the belt and leg loops are attached, spreading the load.

- Gear loops (as if there weren't already enough loops!) are designed to carry equipment such as karabiners, quickdraws, or whatever else you might need for a climb. The more gear loops, the more you can carry.

Diagram labels: Waist belt, Gear loops, Belay loop, Leg loops, Tie-in loops

Be aware...

Because men and women are different shapes (in case you hadn't noticed!), some harnesses are specifically built with that in mind, with a male and female version on the market.

You may also see smaller kids wearing a full body harness. This is because, the younger you are, the bigger your head is compared to the size of your body. A very young child with a GINORMOUS HEAD is much more likely to tip upside down and, without the more prominent hips of their adult counterparts, is likely to fall out of a normal harness. The full-size harness keeps them completely strapped in so there's no chance of escape.

Fitting a harness

The easiest way to put on a harness is to loosen all the straps and then lay it out on the floor in front of you, so that the front of the harness is facing away from you (the bit with the belay loop).

Now, step in into the leg loops and pull the waist belt around your waist so that it sits just over your hips. Although that sounds straight forward, I'll warn you now, the number of times you will step into it and find the leg loops are twisted, the waist belt is upside down, or the leg straps are crossed… Oooooooo, more times than I've had a hot dinners!

Assuming you have pulled the harness up the right way with nothing crossed (except maybe your fingers), then you need to tighten the waist belt. A good rule of thumb is to check the fit by placing your hand flat in between the harness and your body and then making a fist…

If your fist slides out easily, then the fit is likely to be too loose. If you can barely make a fist, it's probably too tight (Mind you, if you have gigantic, KING KONG hands you may wish to take that into consideration)!

Next, tighten each of the leg loops to so that they fit comfortably around your thighs. This time, check that your flat hand (no fist required) fits between your

leg and the harness. You may also be able to adjust the distance between the waist belt and the leg loops. Get into the habit of tucking any dangly bits of strapping out of the way. Many harnesses have elastic loops that you can feed the excess strapping into, so it sits against you rather than potentially getting in the way when you climb.

A good outdoor store will have the ability for you to trial the harness by sitting in it suspended off a length of rope, so that you get to appreciate what it will feel like when you're sitting off the wall taking a rest or being lowered from a climb.

Now, you may wear your climbing shoes so often that they get worn and ragged. Maybe they get a hole in the toe… sure, it's not ideal that your pinkie toe pokes out, but it's not going to seriously affect your safety. I'm not going to go too O.T.T. here… but the same level of wear and tear on a climbing harness could be CATASTROPHIC!!! If you find any cuts, holes, or broken stitching, then send it to the great harness testing station in the sky… kick it into touch… give it a retirement party… (And just to be clear, if you don't know what on earth I'm talking about) … chuck it in the bin! Give it a kiss goodbye, if necessary, but you cannot afford to compromise on safety.

3. Getting roped in… (Rope!)

Yep… rope… it connects a climber (via their harness) to the wall (via the anchor in top roping) as well as to their belayer. It's another pretty essential piece of kit! Now, if you unwisely decided to go climbing using a huge roll of twine, excess washing line, or hosepipe, I'd put money on it breaking… and then you, breaking… on the floor… like a raw egg. Why? Well, clearly the aforementioned items weren't made specifically for climbing. And nor is all rope!

Climbers use DYNAMIC ROPE – a rope that stretches - for climbing. But, why on earth would you want a stretchy bit of rope? Well, it's not elastic band stretchy (that's a bungee cord!), but it does stretch enough to absorb the force generated by a fall. In most circumstances a STATIC ROPE – one that doesn't stretch at all – should not be used for climbing because, if you fall, they are much more likely to snap or injure the climber. It's kind of like the difference between being in a car with your mother when a cat/dog/small child runs out…

- DYNAMIC ROPE MUM calmly applies pressure firmly on the brake until the car comes to a gradual but definite STOP.

- STATIC ROPE MUM slams her foot so hard on the brake the car instantly stops, you're painfully jolted against the seat belt and, everything that's not nailed down, flies through the air and smashes against the windscreen… thanks a lot STATIC ROPE MUM!!!

So, just to be clear: you don't just use 'any old rope' for climbing - it needs to be DYNAMIC and NOT old. But now you have dynamic rope in mind, you will also need to be clear what you want to use it for… top roping, sport climbing, tying up cashiers during a bank robbery, trad climbing, mountaineering, etc.

Climbers have the choice of using SINGLE ROPES, HALF ROPES, or TWIN ROPES. In terms of rope climbing, I've only covered top roping in this book, so let's not 'beat around the bush', if you're going to top rope, you want a single rope.

Single rope

A single rope is just that... one rope. Single rope is used by most climbers indoors and outdoors, particularly for top roping and sport climbing. As you've probably guessed, there are a huge variety of single ropes available on the market, but the key factors to consider are:

i. *Length* - If you intend to climb a 20-metre-high route then don't think a 30-metre rope will be enough! Whatever the length of the climb, you will need AT LEAST double the amount of rope. Most indoor climbing walls are no taller than 12-14 metres, so a 30-metre rope will be sufficient. A longer rope (e.g. 60 metres) may be more appropriate for extended, outdoor routes. But, either way, you must always be sure to check the length of the route BEFORE you attempt to scale it. The last thing you want to do is run out of rope and literally come to the end of the line.

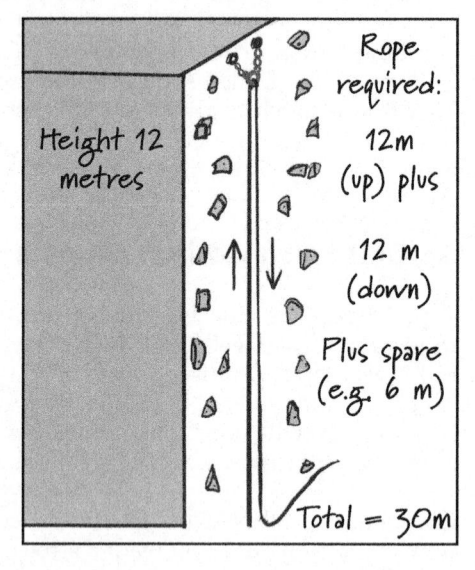

ii. *Thickness* – Generally, single ropes range from 8.9mm – 11 mm in diameter thickness. Considering you are going to trust your life with that rope, 8.9-11 MILLIMETRES might not sound very thick AT ALL! But all legally sold climbing ropes are tested to ensure durability in the event of multiple, bad falls. If you're expecting to really push yourself and fall off a lot, then thicker is better (I could do with a 400mm thick rope the number of times I fall off!).

A 10mm rope is a great one to start out with as it will be hard wearing and easier to use in a belay device than a thinner version (there will be more friction).

Thinner ropes may be preferable if weight is an issue (NOT your weight... the weight of the rope!) as thinner rope is lighter; something to consider if you have to carry it a long way (e.g. to a crag).

iii. *Dry treatment* – If you jumped into a swimming pool with all your clothes you would quickly discover that the material soaks up water, making your clothes heavy and cumbersome. Same with rope: a wet rope is a heavy rope so (a) don't throw it in a swimming pool and (b) based on the conditions in which you are likely to climb, consider whether a rope treated with a water repellent coating might be preferable. So-called 'dry treated' ropes are designed to absorb less water, although will undoubtedly be more expensive. If there's a chance of getting wet, such as climbing in inclement weather, it may be worth the investment. If you're just climbing in perpetually fine weather, then save your cash for a sun hat instead.

iv. *Markings* – Black dye is one means by which some rope manufacturers help you identify the middle and end of a rope. Okay, so you're probably confident that you could already identify the middle and, very definitely, identify the end of the rope without any dye! Fair enough, but middle and end warning markers provide a quick and potentially crucial visual safety guide as to how much rope you have used 'in the system' and how much you might have left.

v. *Safety rating* - All ropes should be appropriately marked with a reputable safety label, such as the Union Internationale des Associations d'Alpinisme (UIAA) and/or a European Norm (EN) standard safety label. This means they have been subject to tests replicating worst-case scenario falls and thereby guaranteeing a high safety standard. If it's not UIAA or EN approved (or an equivalent standard), don't use it - not even to hold up your washing!

vi. *Stretch* - Remember that climbers use DYNAMIC ROPES because they stretch and absorb the force of a fall? Well, you can get more or less stretchy ropes. You want a rope that will E-L-O-N-G-A-T-E enough to absorb the force of a fall, but that's not going to stretch so much that you fall too far! A lower elongation rope tends to be better for top roping. The more of the force or energy the rope absorbs, the less strain it will have on you and your equipment. This is called its IMPACT FORCE (I know, it sounds like a martial arts movie) and is basically the amount of energy/force the rope will absorb. A rope that provides LOWER IMPACT is generally preferable.

"B
U
N
G
E
E
E
Hang on...?
No!
Wait!!!"

Half ropes & Twin ropes

A half rope isn't HALF A ROPE...otherwise it would just be a single rope in half (blimey, now I'm confused!). Half ropes are usually a lot skinnier than single ropes, tend to be used for wandering, multi-pitch trad climbs and are designed to be used in a pair. Yeah, that's right... if you want to use half ropes, you'll need to buy two (a pair of whole halves!?) which will be heavier to carry, although they'll each be skinnier than a single rope. Twin ropes are similarly intended to be used as a pair and are often even skinnier than half ropes...

Let's stop and take a moment... phew... I'd be flabbergasted if you were reading this book intending to get some hints on the best rope for your next complex, multi-pitch trad climb (NEWSFLASH - it ain't going to happen here). So, all you really need to understand is that twin and half ropes EXIST, generally require a higher skill level to use, and have benefits (reduced rope drag, if one gets damaged you have another, you can tie them together for abseiling, etc).

DON'T mix them up with SINGLE ROPE. Accidentally using one rope of a twin rope pair is like going out for a walk in one shoe - it could end in injury!

If it's not obvious from the rope's thickness whether it is single, twin, or half (remember single will generally be 8.9mm or more), single ropes should be marked with a number 1 inside a circle, but, as always, if in doubt, ask an expert.

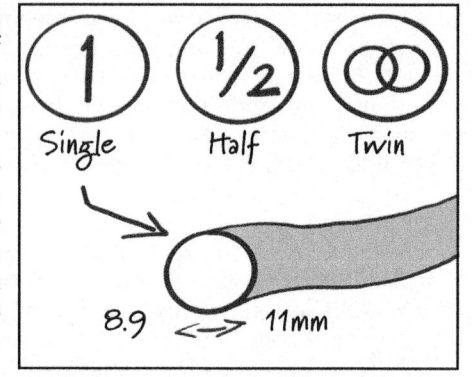

If you're going to suffer the expense of a rope, then make sure you store it in a bag when not in use. Anytime a rope is left on the floor it will pick up dirt which gets engrained in the rope and accelerates the wear. A rope left exposed to direct sunlight can, over time, degrade due to damage from UV light. So, protect it from the elements and it'll last longer.

Everything has a lifespan, which can vary greatly: guinea pigs live about 4 years, rabbits 8-12, giant tortoises 150 years, and the poor old mayfly only lives 24 hours (Can't even watch some Netflix series in that time)! Well, ropes also have an average lifespan, which varies depending on how much usage you get out of it. If you bought a nice new single dynamic rope and kept it in its packaging, some literature suggests it would be good to use for about 10 years.

I'm not sure why you would keep a rope for 10 years before using it, but I think I'd just buy a new one rather than risk it. That said, if you only use the rope occasionally it should comfortably last for several years. If you use it more frequently (e.g. weekly), then it is likely to wear much more quickly (e.g. less than a year). Check the manufacturers guidelines.

But no matter how 'new' your rope might be, if it has been subjected to some major falls, shows signs of wear and tear, or has encountered anything that might damage it (such as chemicals, sharp objects, or a freakishly large hamster with huge gnawing teeth), then consider using it for skipping, a tug of war contest, or for hanging baskets because it's time to replace it. The bottom line is, a rope is a key piece of protective equipment, and you need to check it and maintain it to ensure you can climb safely and confidently.

Finally, whilst you may be able to find second-hand rope or other climbing gear on the internet, it isn't generally recommended. For starters, you'd really want to examine it for wear and tear beforehand, and can you be sure that the equipment that you're trusting with your LIFE has been maintained and looked after?! Personally, I prefer to fork out the extra cash from a reputable store and be able to climb with confidence in my equipment.

"How old did you say this rope was?"

The least you need to know

- There are hard shell (polycarbonate), soft shell (foam), and hybrid (a combination of the two) helmets available on the market. Always wear a climbing specific helmet meeting the industry standard.

- A harness consists of a waist belt, leg loops, belay loops, tie-in loops, and gear loops. The belay loop is the only place you should attach your belay device or an auto-belay karabiner.

- You should use a single rope for top rope climbing and, before purchase, consider the following features: length, thickness, dry treatment, markings, safety rating, and stretch.

- Discard any equipment that is damaged or showing signs of wear such as a cracked helmet, torn harness, old or frayed rope – your life is worth much more than the cost of a replacement.

11

THE GREAT OUTDOORS?
TAKING THE FIRST STEPS CLIMBING OUTDOORS

> If you're anything like me, leisure time is in short supply. Indoor climbing gyms are hugely convenient because, within a relatively small area, you will find multiple routes, all clearly marked in terms of difficulty. Minutes after arriving, you can bound up one after another without so much as a break and, as soon as you decide to finish, you zip up your bag and you're out the door! Whilst a great deal of climbers will be happy to solely stick with indoor climbing forever, many also venture outdoors. What you should come to realise on reading this chapter is that going climbing outdoors is not quite as straightforward.
>
> Whilst bouldering focused, this chapter will provide you with an understanding of outdoor climbing considerations relevant to all types of climbing, including:
>
> - What you should pack and prepare before you venture outdoors.
> - The different challenges of climbing outdoors on 'real' rock.
> - How to use the natural crack in a rock for an ascent (crack climbing).

Indoor vs Outdoor climbing – Aren't they just the same thing?

Ironically it can be the artificial element to indoor climbing that puts some people off. Can you have a true adventure inside a purpose-built climbing gym compared to the GREAT OUTDOORS? Isn't an indoor climbing wall simply a reproduction of the real thing?

Certainly, they both involve climbing, but there are key differences you need to consider before you make the leap. The main one for me being: when you go climbing outdoors there are no climbing staff to watch over you, provide advice, point out an issue, or come to your aid (unless you have arranged otherwise!). So, whilst you may FEEL confident in your knowledge, skills, and ability as a climber, it's essential that you ACTUALLY ARE! There is no room for error!

The other strikingly obvious difference is that there's unlikely to be a nice coffee shop which does cheese toasties and fudge cake, tea making facilities, snack machines, handy lockers, toilets, or changing rooms in the wilderness. Any creature comforts you might want, you're most likely going to have to carry there yourself!

What to pack

Must have essentials include:

- **A buddy**
- **Water**
- **Grub (food)**
- **First aid kit**
- **Sturdy footwear**
- **Waterproof clothing**
- **Phone & battery pack**
- **Map**
- **Guidebook**
- **Climbing equipment**

A buddy

Okay, so I don't mean you're going to have to force your friend into a duffel bag, but I am serious when I suggest that you should plan to go with someone. Have you seen the film 127 hours?! SPOILER ALERT – It's the true story about Aron Ralston who, whilst out solo climbing in the middle of nowhere, got a limb trapped by a dislodged boulder. No one knew where he was, he had no mobile phone (there was no reception anyway), and he would most certainly have died had he not self-performed a gruesome operation. Things needn't be that complicated. Even if you're confident in your own ability, there is always the possibility of injury, so go climbing with a buddy.

A trained outdoor instructor or climbing coach would be rather handy, but unless you know one, then try and go with someone who has climbed outdoors before. And failing that, a friend or family member. And failing that... you could always ask the postie or refuse collector if they fancy a day trip?!

More water than you think you'll need.

The last time I tried to go all 'rugged survivalist', I drank a pint of 'fresh water' from a stream. I was happy enough until I discovered the rotting carcass of a dead sheep further upstream... mmmmm, a taste of the country! No rotting sheep carcasses in my kitchen sink though, so that's where I fill up now.

Bear in mind that every litre of water you take is another kilo of weight to carry. But there's no room for scrimping - one water bottle isn't going to cut it for a day or even half day. Better to carry as much as possible than find yourself completely parched, licking the dew off leaves to survive.

If you are going to be completely off the beaten track, then a purpose-built hydration bladder mightn't be a bad investment either; the kind with a drinking hose that fits into your rucksack. It means you can get take a gulp of fluid whenever you desire, rather than toting around multiple bottles and having to unpack half your wardrobe just to 'wet your whistle'.

Grub

Unless you're planning on nibbling roots and berries or trapping and killing the local wildlife, stuffing your bag full of tasty treats is a MUST. You're going to burn calories walking to and from the 'crag', let alone when you start climbing, so make sure you pack sufficient energy sustaining foods to keep you going all the way there, and all the way home. For example, a bag of homemade trail mix made up of nuts, seeds, and berries provides a lightweight and nutritious snack.

I'd recommend carrying any food in hardy sealed containers. Alternatively, follow my lead by bringing sandwiches to inadvertently sit on, a flimsy pot of pasta to pop open in your bag, or my personal favourite, something made with oil, juice, or sauce just ready to leak over absolutely everything else!

First aid kit

I know you're not planning to hurt yourself, but it pays to have a few, "just in case" handy items tucked away: plasters are always a good bet because, 'Sod's law' dictates, someone will either get a blister walking to the crag, graze their knee on a rock, or get bitten by a vicious creepy crawly. Dare I say it, but a handful of sterile bandages are also worthwhile in case of something worse! And antihistamines will be crucial if you suddenly discover a previously unknown allergy to animal, insect, flora, or fauna.

Obviously, if you need them, bring your own prescription meds, but also bung in your own selection of drugstore supplies such as antiseptic creams, paracetamol, rehydration salts, and anti-diarrhoea meds (I mean... if you're about to poo yourself inside out, could there be a worse place to be than halfway up a rockface?!).

And it never harms to have some instant ice packs – little pouches that you bash to create a chemical reaction, providing 20 or so minutes of cold. Unless you happen to be ice climbing, ice or anything vaguely resembling a cold compress is, unsurprisingly, in short supply in the countryside, but an absolute requirement for sprained limbs (particularly ankles on all that uneven ground, with a walk home to boot).

Oh NO! He's allergic to fresh air!

Sturdy footwear

The walk on the way to a climbing destination is, at least in some climbing communities, referred to as the 'approach'. Having a sturdy pair of shoes for the walk is crucial. All I'd say is walking to a crag is going play hell with your high heels, so invest in a decent pair of walking shoes that are rough and tough enough for your journey.

Many outdoor stores specifically sell 'approach shoes'. These are often billed as shoes somewhere between a hiking boot and a climbing shoe, with features that are better suited to scrambling over rock. They tend to be lighter and stiffer than a hiking boot but considerably more comfortable than a climbing shoe. Approach shoes are probably a good call if you are likely to be walking or scrambling over rocky terrain to the bottom of a mountain crag, but unlikely to add much value at a rocky outcrop next to the main road or at the edge of a beach. Incidentally, you won't find 'departure shoes', 'get back in the car shoes', or 'at home planning my next trip shoes', although there may be a market for them... (I'm currently wearing my 'being facetious shoes').

Whose coat is that jacket? (Additional clothing)

Outdoor pursuits with the wind in your hair...

Look out of the window and you will quickly come to realise that the weather has an ENORMOUS impact on your ability to go outdoor climbing. You know when your parents used to irritatingly say, "You can't put on what you haven't brought...", "You won't feel the benefit...", "You'll catch your death in those...", etc... etc...

Well, turns out they were right! Pack extra layers, whatever the weather, and always bring a waterproof... if you don't, it's bound to rain!

A phone

Whilst a mobile phone may be useful to take a bucketload of selfies on your adventure, it'll also be handy if you get lost or need help. But mobile phones are of NO USE WHATSOEVER when they run out of battery (you know – from taking all those unnecessary selfies), so make sure it is fully charged or bring a battery pack or two to 'juice up' when required. Also, be aware, contrary to what your mobile phone provider might tell you, there are huge areas of countryside with NO RECEPTION, so don't completely rely on your phone being able to connect you with the outside world.

One very worthwhile app to consider getting downloaded on your phone is What3words. The designers divided the world into 3 metre squares and gave each square a unique combination of three words. So, for example:

ROCK. PAPER. SCISSORS is near Vicuna in South America.
ROCK. PAPER. ACID is near Fitzgerald Street, North Perth, Western Australia.
WORK. PAPER. ACID is near Basingstoke canal, Aldershot, UK.

Even if you're in the middle of the mountains, forest, desert, or sea (sea climbing?), the app provides your location within a 3-metre square area. It's so precise it is used by emergency services around the world to help and find people in need. Hopefully that won't be you, but if it is, then at least you can be confident in the knowledge that help is coming (Assuming you have reception... and your battery hasn't run out from taking selfies).

I did search I. AM. LOST but, somewhat ironically, that combination isn't mapped (perhaps to put off people like me searching for it).

Map

Of course, technically you shouldn't need a phone or get lost if you have a map. Print a map of the intended climbing area off the internet, or go completely crazy, and just buy one! It doesn't mean you're turning into your grandfather; it just means you will be less likely to get COMPLETELY and UTTERLY LOST.

Which brings me on to my second map-related tip (you can thank me later): LOOK AT IT BEFORE YOU ACTUALLY LEAVE (I know, I know... this book provides some astounding insights)! Reading a map isn't always straight forward, especially if you haven't had practice. Take a bit of time to work out your route to the crag and don't assume you're going to be sauntering down a nice flat pathway. Contours = steepness. What might look like a leisurely quarter mile stroll, could be a gruelling slog up terrain that would do well in an Everest lookalike competition.

Guidebook

You may have realised by now that climbing outdoors requires a bit more thought and planning compared to climbing indoors. The great thing about outdoor rock climbing is that, unless you're about to go bouldering on the surface of the moon, generally someone, somewhere will have written a guidebook describing the climbing in any given area. So, wherever you are thinking of going climbing, it is also advisable to purchase a guidebook/app and save yourself a lot of time and energy in the interim. It isn't much fun going to the effort of packing all your climbing gear, travelling to an unfamiliar location, and realising you don't have a clue where to start.

The better guides will not only describe the type and grade of the climbing routes located in the area, but also the best means of travelling to a crag, parking, the approach, the condition of the crag (e.g. sunny location, overgrown, etc), local amenities and, if you're lucky, will provide colour photographs of the actual routes so you can be absolutely sure you're in the right place. Believe me, unless you happen to have aerial imagery from a passing satellite, trying to find the correct 'rock' in the middle of the countryside is no easy feat.

Beware: some guidebooks are written solely, or in the main, describing trad routes (remember - you place your own climbing 'protection' along the route) as opposed to bouldering, top rope, or sport climbing. Your first clue, other than the title being, 'TRAD CLIMBING GUIDE', is a totally unexpected grade system, such as the British Grading System that, to a newcomer, will seem utterly bizarre, using terms such as HD (Hard Difficult), HVS (Hard Very Severe) and ES (extremely severe).

Climbing equipment

Whatever you intend to do, you're going to require all the equipment that would be essential as if you were climbing indoors... and more:

Rope climbing

A helmet, harness, belay device, karabiner, and rope are the absolute minimum requirements. There are limitless opportunities for rope climbing outdoors. However, although there is likely to be some top rope climbing, most climbs will either be sport (fixed bolts on a cliff that a climber clips their rope into) or trad routes (where you place your own safety equipment). The level of knowledge required just to set up a safe rope system for top rope falls outside the scope of this book (If this book sells more copies than the one to my parents, a couple of friends, and a bloke who accidentally dropped it in his Amazon basket then, who knows, perhaps I'll write a guide on it). But although you may be tempted to just give rope climbing outdoors a whirl, especially with the benefit of the internet – I mean there's going to be a million and one posts about it after all - just hold that thought:

I learnt how to change the oil filter in my car by watching a YouTube video. I can't remember how to do it now and, as my car hasn't exploded, I'm kind of assuming that I did it correctly. But, even if I'd followed the YouTube video guide incorrectly, the worst situation I'd have is a car with an oil filter problem. Get something wrong after following a YouTube video about climbing and you could fall to your death or accidentally kill someone. Not a fabulous combination! There are a huge array of YouTube videos providing instruction on a wide range of topics, including climbing. A significant percentage of these videos are made by absolute donuts! So even if you did follow them to the letter, you still might fall to your death or accidentally kill someone! I have a very simple message. You've heard it before. Sorry to be boring: get instruction from a professional instructor or someone with proven (outdoor) climbing experience. Your life is worth the investment!

Bouldering

Indoor bouldering areas have soft matting to help break a fall. No such luxuries available in the wilderness. So, if you're planning on bouldering outdoors, you're also going to need a 'boulder mat'; basically, a portable and durable crash pad that you can fall onto. It may be tempting to save some money and use, for example, the cushions off your mum's sofa (I have seen that at a crag more than once!), but, whilst comfortable to sit on (that's what they're designed for after all), cushions (your mum's or otherwise) are unlikely to protect you. Bouldering mats, on the other hand, are made of double or triple density foam with a very high absorption capacity so that a climber can safely fall on them again and again. Furthermore, carrying an assortment of sofa cushions is going to be tricky, impossible to clean, and your mum is probably going to kill you.

Boulder mats usually have shoulder straps so that you can carry them on your back like a rucksack, or front… or both, so that you become the MEAT between the BUNS! There is a rich selection of boulder mats on the market, but generally get the thickest and biggest one you think you can conceivably carry to the crag. When you're balanced at the top of the boulder and suddenly slip, you want to guarantee you land on the mat, rather than the floor, your mate, or passing wildlife.

I accept, falling off a boulder may not sound such an issue if you're bouldering on, say, sand; but if you're bouldering in an area where there are lots of rocks, then a fall could prove serious. Also, it makes sense to go bouldering with as many boulder mats as you can possibly carry, so you can cover the 'fall zone' with as much protection as possible. Alternatively befriend as many people as you can and get them to carry them!

Above all, make sure you bring your climbing shoes! Honestly... tie them around your waist. Nothing quite like going outdoor climbing and realising you've left them in the cupboard at home!

PACKED and ready to go? Before you leave:

TELL SOMEONE where you are going. And not just anyone... It is wise to tell someone who is (a) listening, (b) you can trust to remember, and (c) is sensible enough to react if you don't return within a reasonable time. And failing that, write your destination on the fridge. When the police come searching, they will at least have one significant clue to follow up!

Secondly, and whilst not quite as important (although it could be as messy if you get it wrong): make sure you've been to toilet!!! Jean and Gladys, the cleaning ladies, come into the climbing gym every morning to hoover the chalk off the mats, flush away any NASTY CHOCOLATE SURPRISES in the toilet block, and generally give everything a thorough going over. Outdoor climbing environments rely on the user (that means YOU buddy) ensuring that no damage is caused to the area by leaving rubbish (including chalk dust), trampling the vegetation, or weeing/pooing all over the place! Fact of the matter is many great crags are situated in beautiful countryside, so plan to make as little impact as possible: LEAVE ONLY FOOTPRINTS.

ROOOOOOAD TRIP! (Travelling to the crag)

Outdoor rock formations offer a huge range of climbs for different levels of ability, but generally without the high number of people that you might encounter during peak times at an indoor gym. Although, on a nice day, popular crags can also get busy. Few outdoor venues can cope with much vehicular traffic and, given that there aren't likely to be any multi-storey car parks (thankfully), parking may be limited to a few spaces. So, if you can cycle or walk then consider it part of your warm-up! If not, establish whether you can get public transport (Although, be aware, the bus conductor is NOT going to be happy with you trying to push through a crowded coach carrying boulder mats on your back).

If you're driving or cadging a lift off your friend or parent in a car/bus/banana boat don't just rely on the SATNAV getting you there. I have found – TO MY HORROR – that the SAT NAV's interpretation of a 'road' was vastly different to mine (Cue hideous memory of me quivering in fear as I edged along a potholed, dirt track with an occasional fence post demarking the road between me and a 1000-foot drop)! Again, a good ole fashioned map may be the answer if you're heading to an unfamiliar wilderness area.

If there is a carpark, use it! I know you'll be keen to get out and get climbing, but not everyone is going to look favourably on carloads of climbers parking on every available verge, nook, and cranny as far as the eye can see.

Generally, the more popular the climbing area, the easier it's going to be to find. There may be signposting or notices, and you might even be able to rely on passers-by for direction. For less travelled routes, whilst it may be obvious to a Native American tracker or your stereotypical weathered old explorer, finding the right pathway can be tricky. Be prepared to dump your stuff and scout ahead. If you find yourself walking along a huge expanse of grassland and the only thing for miles is an enormous rock towering into the sky, then it's a safe bet that that's where the climbing is going to be. But not all crags are quite so obvious. And what you DON'T want to do is inadvertently wander off the top of one!

"He said he wanted to be at one with nature...

Now he's part of the crag!"

Routing 4 u

Identifying the right climbing route for you

Assuming you make it to the crag alive, the next thing you going to want to do – well, after throwing all your stuff on the ground (!) – is have a good walk about to get your bearings, identify any potential hazards and, if necessary, WEAR PROTECTION (Dude... I mean a HELMET!). Remember: outdoor crags haven't been vigorously safety checked... bits can drop off... and when I say "bits", I mean ROCKS. A dislodged rock falling on your head may turn the trip of a lifetime to the trip of the last time.

If you've bought a guidebook (and remembered to pack it!) or downloaded an app, take some time to check out the routes.

Even matching a description, drawing, or picture in a book or app to the actual rock face can be a challenge. Individual boulders, rocks, and even cliffs can look pretty darn similar. So don't be surprised if you find yourself pacing round trying to determine via the location, shape, and surface of various rock formations whether you've got the right one!

Be advised: Guides can NOT account for nature disguising routes through natural occurrences such as sprouting undergrowth or rockfall.

"I'm sure it was supposed to be around here."

With indoor climbing, what grade of difficulty a route receives is often decided by 'a consensus of route setters' (bit like a school of whales, only smaller). This can vary quite dramatically from gym to gym.

Cynics may claim that some climbing gyms elevate the grade setting, just to make everyone feel a bit better about their climbing, thereby ensuring a continuing flow of revenue. If your climbing gym is guilty of such a heinous crime, you'll soon find out when trialling other climbing locations.

"I've just topped a 9B on my warm-up!"

ACME KIDS PARTY CLIMBS

Outdoor route difficulty is more likely to have been assigned by the first person to climb it (or record they climbed it), or the author of the guidebook documenting the route. It follows then, that in the same way indoor route grades are very subjective, outdoor route grading can also vary quite a bit. In fact, outdoor route difficulty can change daily. Several factors contribute to this, the weather being a significant dynamic. Whilst it might be obvious that, if it's pouring down with rain, a route is going to be significantly more difficult, what's not so widely appreciated is that even slight changes in humidity or heat can affect the ability to GRIP the rock. Also, as rock ages and is subject to erosion or degradation from constant climbing, holds that may once have been relatively good become worn down, broken, or polished, making them more difficult to grip.

If you're lucky, each route will be a couple of metres apart… alternatively they may be significantly spaced. And a relatively easy route may be next to an astronomically difficult one. You need to make sure you know which one is which before you start, because they certainly won't be labelled. And bear in mind, there are conceivably still undiscovered routes, the sort that an Indiana Jones climber equivalent would search for, which aren't graded at all.

Whatever you chose, your previous reliance on BRIGHTLY COLOURED HOLDS to demark your route will become all too apparent. You may find it difficult to see the route at all! Outdoor climbing is where reading a route comes into its own, because if you can't work out where the holds are, you're not going anywhere fast! The fact that you must search for the holds is appealing to some who enjoy this extra dimension to their climbing. Others find it extraordinarily challenging and can become so irritated by their inability to read the route, that they basically sack the idea of outdoor climbing altogether. Stick with it! You will soon come to realise that nature knows no bounds - there is an infinite variety of holds and features on outdoor walls; you just need to unlock each puzzle.

"Is this a difficult route?"

Ground nesting boulderer

Prepare your area for safe bouldering

Once you've identified the route you want to climb, you need to 'set up' with SAFETY as your prerogative. Bringing boulder mats is one thing, but should you fall, you want to make sure you actually land on them! Chucking a boulder mat haphazardly at the base of the climb won't necessarily guarantee a HAPPY LANDING. So, first things first, decide on the best place to put your mat(s) and, if you have a spotter, settle on where they're going to stand/move. And then clear the area of everything else:

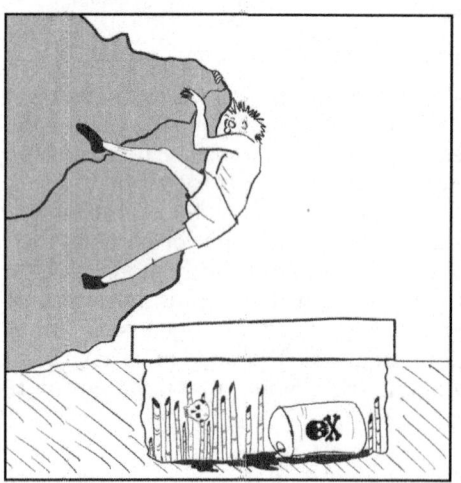

Bags, water bottles, your grandma's knitting needles... anything that's going to become a potential trip hazard or the worst kind of landing pad in the event of a fall. There are likely to be some natural hazards that you can't physically move out of the way like rocks, trees, animal burrows, bushes, and my absolute nemesis, the dreaded tree root – a trip hazard of unfeasible magnitude. Stacking boulder mats over potential nasties is a good option, although beware of gaps between mats. Falling down the crack between two boulder mats is a surefire way of twisting an ankle!

It's important that you work out where the climber is likely to fall during their route. Although they may happily land on the mats from a fall at the start of the climb, the route may take them completely out of the original fall zone. The climber may move left, right, or in the case of an overhang, behind the first mat placement as they progress along it. Somewhat akin to firefighters moving a giant net to catch a jumper from a burning building, a spotter has to move the mat where the climber is most likely to land at any one point. This generally requires a lot of hasty mat shuffling, whilst trying to keep one eye on the climber.

Spotting really does take on a whole new meaning when you're doing it outdoors. An occasional lapse of concentration in an indoor setting may result in your climbing partner falling and landing awkwardly... on soft matting.

Outdoors, they might miss the boulder mat altogether and land on a rock! Whatever friendship or bond of trust you have developed, if you fail in your spotting duty you are likely to be FOREVER remembered as the guy/gal that's, "...a great spotter, except for this one time... blah, blah, blah..." (regurgitate old war story about climber hitting the dirt!).

Remember, the job of a spotter is to guide a falling climber to safety, so keep your eyes firmly on the task and, if required, forcefully move your climbing partner out the way of a hazard; ideally without falling on top of it yourself!

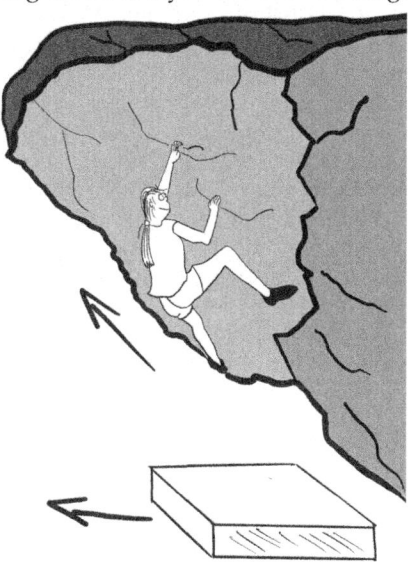

Exposing yourself(!) ...to the outdoors

'Exposure' in an outdoor environment can be scary and unpleasant. You'll be thankful I'm not referring to the type of exposure that involves a seedy old man in a long mac, but rather the feeling you might get as a climber outside on real rock. After having been used to the warm, comfortable, and controlled environment of an indoor climbing gym, climbing out in the open brings with it a plethora of new sensations: the breeze on your face, the gritty feel of rock, the hardness of the ground, the sound of birds, or conversely, the total silence. When you add to this the fact that you'll be trying to decipher a route that isn't clearly marked, the complete and utter 'openness' of your surroundings can be overwhelming.

The very worst exposure

I vividly remember being stuck on what I believed to be an easy boulder problem (I would have used the equivalent graded climb indoors as a warm-up). It was a windy day and each gust felt like it was trying to push me off the wall. Frustrated, I was already a little shaken after my hand had slipped on the build-up of grit on a hold. I'd been balanced on a ledge for so long that my calf muscles were burning.

"There aren't any handholds!" I moaned, a complaint you will hear alot from climbers new to the outdoors. I was acutely aware that if I slipped, which seemed increasingly likely, I would fall. But the boulder mat seemed a lot smaller and further away than I seemed to remember. As my anxiety increased, I became more desperate, blindly slapping my hand over the surface of the rock, disturbing a spider that had been tucked in a nook. It may well have been the world's smallest and friendliest spider but, as it ran out of the nook towards my hand, I squealed like a three-year-old at a birthday party, and promptly fell off the ledge.

Although clearly not my finest hour, the incident very firmly underlined that my performance expectations were set too high. It's natural to be anxious. You should not underestimate the additional factors your brain has to process when climbing outdoors and the stress or anxiety that this can create. It can also be frustrating because it's likely you felt you'd got through such feelings when you started climbing in an indoor setting. Be patient... you are, after all, learning a whole new component of climbing. Simply accept it as another stage in your climbing journey.

Spot the difference

Outdoor vs indoor climbing

Here are a few tips that may help prepare you for your outdoor climb:

- **Do not** expect to turn up and smash the same grade of route that you will have completed indoors. You're going to climb on NATURAL ROCK and, depending on what it is – limestone, granite, basalt, slate, sandstone, etc – it will have an altogether different texture to the relatively standard resin or wooden holds found in indoor rock gyms.

- **Explore** the rock face with your eyes, but don't just stare at the rock directly in front of you: look above, below, and either side of your line of sight. Use your hands to feel around for anything that might give you more purchase on the wall. When nature itself is the route setter, you must adapt, be creative, bolder, and braver with your moves.

- **Look** at where the best holds for your hands are.... And DON'T FORGET to look at the best holds for your feet as well! It can be a lot harder working out your footing when everything is the same 'rock' colour. Don't be afraid to take much smaller steps than you might expect to at an indoor wall. And lots of them... It's remarkable how even gaining a tiny bit of height on the wall can suddenly provide a myriad of holds that you wouldn't have seen or otherwise reached.

- **Remember**: many outdoor companies have spent a huge amount of time, scientific research, and energy to engineer climbing shoes with rubber that grips the tiniest dimple in the rock, so learn to TRUST YOUR FEET!

- **Be aware** that temperature and humidity can have a big impact on the amount of friction generated between your fingers and the holds. If it's hot and humid, you may find you're slip-sliding all over the shop. Climb the same route in colder, drier weather and suddenly you're stuck to the wall like chewing gum on your mum's new carpet!

- **Be prepared** to call it a day. You may have invested time and energy getting to your crag but the weather may be the defining factor in whether the day is a success or disaster! Climbing in strong winds, or on wet or icy rock, is MUCH more hazardous than the nice dry, airconditioned inside of a climbing gym, and frankly isn't much fun! Better to return on a nice day rather than put yourself off for life!

A cracking discovery

Brief introduction to crack climbing

A little while ago I dropped a cup. Luckily, I dropped it on the dog (NOT ON PURPOSE – before you report me to 'Animal Welfare')! Anyway, it bounced off the dog (who, to be fair, wasn't that fussed because she thought it was food) and then onto the floor. "Phew!" I exclaimed, thankful it hadn't broken into pieces. I soon became as annoyed as the dog (who, by this time was quite put out, having realised I hadn't dropped food after all), because when I picked it up, I discovered a giant crack down the side. The crack was an obvious line of weakness on the cup - it could split and break at any point - and was of little further use. I did what any normal, adult male would do… I put it at the back of the cupboard so my wife wouldn't find out!

BOO to cracks heh?!

Well, yes and no… because, as it happens, cracks on a rock face can be a climber's best friend. And I'm not just talking about little itsy splits in the rock; I'm talking GIANT 1 metre, 5 metre, 10 metre, 20 metre, 30 metre, 40 metre, 50 metre (… okay, you get the point) CRACKS that can span the height of the rock face and which are entirely usable as a means of progressing an ascent.

Indoor climbing gyms generally just use bolt-on holds, although some may install a crack route: this will generally be an indentation within the surface of the climbing wall or a ready-made, angled hold shaped like a fissure. Although worthy of exploration, you are much, much, much more likely to need to get to grips with crack climbing outdoors, where there is an infinite variety on offer.

A technique essential to crack climbing is called JAMMING. It has nothing to do with Bob Marley (ask anyone over 40) or sitting around with your mates strumming tunes on your guitar. Jamming involves squashing your fingers, hands, or feet into a crack.

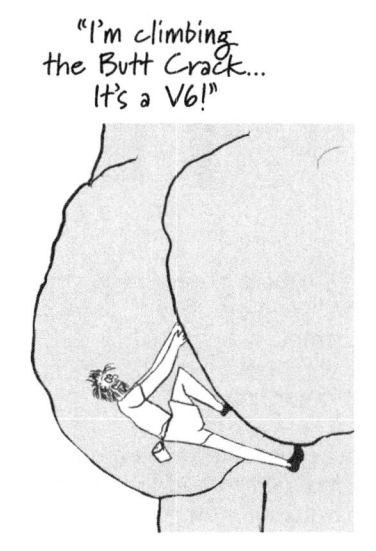

Frankly, there's nothing stopping you wedging any body part in, but bear in mind if you get stuck, you better hope the ladder on the Firefighters' truck is long enough to reach you. You've probably heard about some kid getting their head caught between the bars of a fence, so purposefully squashing any part of your body into a gap in the rock might seem somewhat counterintuitive. But in the absence of a hold, jamming is a proven mechanism of ascent.

Effective jamming is not only physically demanding but can be quite painful. The trick is to place your jam and then keep it in position as you move up the wall. It goes without saying – remove all jewellery before crack climbing. If you don't, it is likely to get OBLITERATED on the rock and you risk serious injury. The main types of jam are:

Fist jam

Place your hand into the crack and form a fist with your thumb on one side and little finger on the other. Clench your fist and the pressure will lock your hand in place. Rather than risk abrasing your knuckles, the soft parts of your fist should act as a wedge. You can fist jam with your palm up or down.

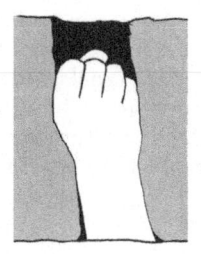

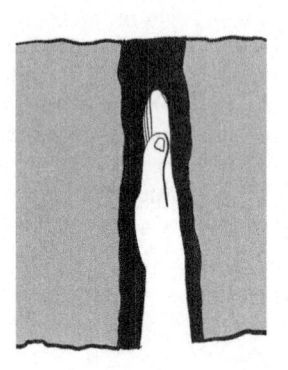

Palm down　　*Palm up*

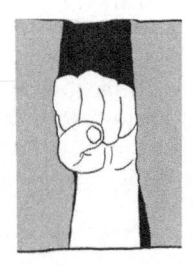

Hand jam

Place your flat hand into the crack. Then, cup your hand, squeezing your thumb into your palm. The heel of you palm, back of your hand, and fingertips will similarly lock your hand in place.

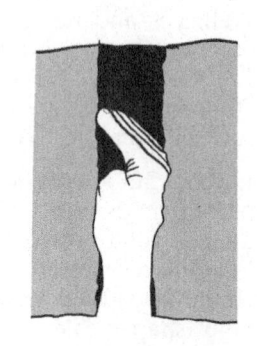

Of course, some cracks are going to be way too small to use your hand, requiring instead, the cunningly named...

Finger jam

In general terms, it requires you to insert your fingers into a crack and then twist, like a key in the lock. The choice of exactly which fingers is going to be down

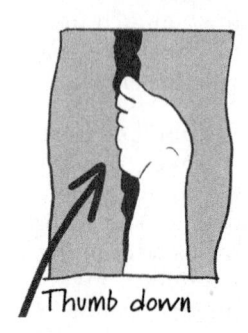

Thumb down

to the size of the crack and what feels comfortable (bearable!) to you. It's going to take time to feel confident enough to rely on, say, a squashed ring finger and pinkie to hold you to the side of a cliff.

Jamming takes practice and a few scrapes here and there are inevitable. No one will want to follow you on a crack climb if it's covered in torn skin and a trail of blood, so, in preparation for a significant crack climb, it's not a bad idea to tape your hands. This will provide some protection for your skin. You can limit this to your knuckles or go the whole hog and make a tape glove!

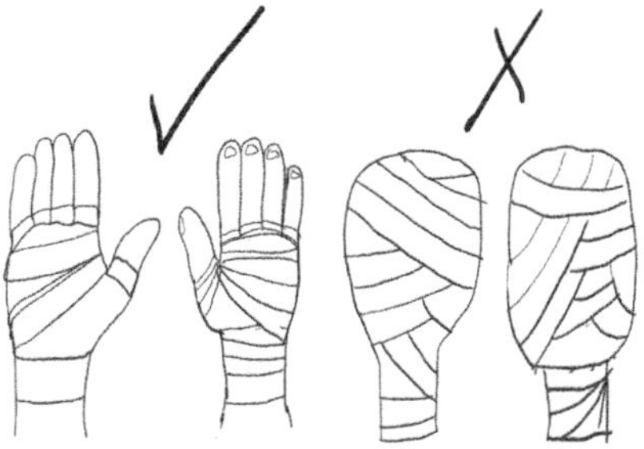

Pull down to lock into place

Sticky sports tape comes in a variety of sizes, but a rule of thumb (or rather, a rule of fingers and thumb) is to use tape with a width of about 0.25-0.75 inches for your fingers (and thumb!!!) and wider tape – anywhere between 1-2 inches - for your hands.

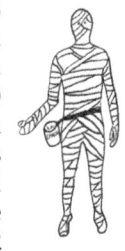

Hand and fist jams are the staple diet of a crack climber. And it follows that, if you can successfully squash either into a crack, then you SHOULD also be able to use the same crack for your foot.

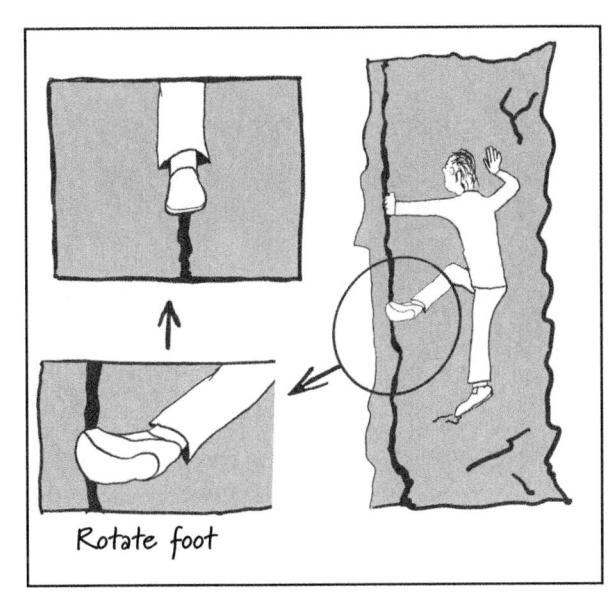

Rotate foot

Foot jam

A foot jam can be relatively easily achieved by placing your foot, sideways into a crack, with your big toe facing up.

Turn the sole of your shoe down and as long as the crack isn't wider than the width of your foot, it should hold firmly... well for most people anyway!

The least you need to know

- Plan to climb outdoors with a companion and make sure you pack sufficient food and water, as well as other essentials, such as a first aid kit, extra clothing layers, a fully charged phone, and a map or guidebook. And don't forget your shoes!!!

- If you're planning on bouldering, take at least one good quality boulder mat, but more if possible. Scan the climbing area/landing zone for hazards and, if spotting, be prepared to move the climber away from danger.

- Manage your performance expectations – climbing outdoors is an altogether different experience. Factors such as route and hold identification, weather, exposure, and wildlife will all impact your climbing.

- Natural rock will look and feel very different to the resin or wood holds in an indoor climbing gym. Take your time to read the route and explore the rock face through touch, as well as searching with your eyes, for the best hand and footholds available.

- Climbers use the natural cracks on a rock face to ascend via use of a hand, fist, finger, or foot jam. Taping the hands will help protect against injury.

12

IN DEEP WATER:
DEEP WATER SOLOING/PSICOBLOC

Deep Water Soloing (DWS) or Psicobloc generally involves climbing above water outdoors. There are two seriously important additional skills any budding climber requires before considering going:

The first and by far the MOST IMPORTANT is the ability to swim. The clue is in the title: IN DEEP WATER. If you fall in, the only way out is to swim. If you can't swim, then give DWS a miss... or learn to swim.

The second key skill is the ability to fall from height into potentially freezing cold water in your clothes, without being put off climbing forever!

If you believe you possess these additional abilities, then I am delighted to inform you that DWS can be both fun and thrilling. This chapter will provide you with an understanding of:

- What to pack.
- Additional factors to consider before you literally 'take the plunge'.
- Climbing above water grade system.
- How to fall!

Wet fish

Additional kit

DWS can give climbers a huge feeling of freedom: climbing above water with no kit other than your climbing shoes (and ideally some swimwear). But, over and above the list of gear to bring outdoor climbing (see Chapter 11 'The Great Outdoors?'), there are some additional kit considerations:

- Solid or powder chalk is going to be NAFF ALL use wet. So, consider packing a chalk bag that you have lined with another plastic bag and place the chalk in that. If the chalk gets wet, you can simply replace the inner plastic bag with a refill. Also, think about packing some liquid chalk as well. Not that you're going to want to be carrying a bottle to squirt on your hands mid route. But, either give them a good covering before you start the route or squirt some extra along your skin (e.g. forearm or thigh) so that you can rub your fingers over the surplus in times of need/desperation.

- A plastic bin liner is a good idea. You should have realised by now that water is WET(!) and you may have to move through it before, during, or after a climb. A plastic bin liner will keep your clothes and gear dry if you move through water at any point, and it's equally handy to chuck wet stuff into at the end of the day.

- DWS tends to be done in nice weather. So, if there's a chance that you're going to be exposing parts of your body that rarely see the sun (I mean like your back – yearggh! What did you think?!), then suntan lotion is a must. Earning yourself a red back from a bad landing is bad enough, but getting an ultra-red back from a bad landing on sun burn is going to sting like you've struck a bed of vipers!

- Lotions aside, protracted exposure to the water may cool your body right down - a flask of hot tea, coffee, or chocolate can be an instant and welcome way to warm the cockles!

- This may sound obvious… and it is, but: PACK SPARE CLOTHES. Pretty much NOTHING is fun when you are cold and wet, let alone climbing whilst cold and wet. Even if it's burning hot in the sun when you start out, the weather changes (like the weather!) and you don't want to end the day wet, cold, and miserable, so bring enough layers that you can chuck them on when at will (e.g. when you're sitting/standing around between climbs).

- Do you really want to wear your best climbing shoes if there's a possibility that they're going to get soaked? DWS presents an ideal opportunity to use any old or worn shoes, where water damage isn't a concern.

- If you're seriously nervous about falling into the water, then you could always consider taking a suitable floatation device. I'm not saying you need to wear water wings and a rubber hoop around your waist, but anything that will help keep you up in the water might be a bonus. Okay, so it's going to get in the way during climbing and you're unlikely to achieve the rugged free climber look, but then you won't look too cool flapping around in the water requiring rescue either.

- Coastal areas tend not to have the best mobile phone coverage, and of course, a wet phone is no good to anyone. Make sure your mobile phone and any portable charger is sealed in a waterproof bag, and ensure you have a number for the Coastguard stored on it.

Taking the plunge

Additional factors to consider

Although going with 'a buddy' has already been covered in Chapter 11, it goes without saying: if you can go with a professional climbing instructor, DWS guide, or someone who has experience of DWS, then do so. There are many additional hazards above and below water, and whilst you may be able to safely navigate them, you are much more likely to have an enjoyable, less stressful, and safer experience with the benefit of some additional expertise on hand. Certainly, I would only advise going to a known DWS area, as opposed to finding and deciding to go climbing in an area over water.

Purchasing a Deep Water Soloing specific guidebook is a REALLY good idea.

With any body of water, there may be dangers that mightn't be obvious until it's too late, such as strong currents, poisonous marine animals, or rocks below the surface.

A good guidebook should detail the difficulty of available routes, hazards, as well as the best approach routes and exit points.

Landing zone

When you Deep Water Solo, the water is going to act as a giant boulder mat equivalent. However, unlike a boulder mat, there may be unseen hazards lurking just beneath the surface. If you hit a rock underneath the water it's going to REALLY, REALLY, hurt! (That's why there's no such thing as HARD CONCRETE SOLOING or PILE OF BROKEN GLASS SOLOING). And spraining or breaking a limb in deep water could be even more perilous than if it happened on land.

So, in the same way you would scan an area for the best boulder mat placement, it's worth scoping the drop zone beneath your intended route. If you think it will help determine the risk, stick on a pair of goggles and dunk your head under, or go one further and swim beneath the route beforehand. It will allow you to identify the risky spots and may also help to determine the best way of exiting the water in the event of a fall.

"Tidy?" - DWS and the influence of tides

When climbing in any coastal area you're also going to have to think about TIDES. The sea level constantly rises and falls, and so it's important to know when the water is at its highest point (HIGH TIDE), when there should be plenty of water depth, compared to when the water is at its lowest point (LOW TIDE), when you might unknowingly be SHALLOW WATER SOLOING (not a recognised or advisable pastime). In some areas, the difference in water depth will be barely perceptible, but in others, water depth can change by many metres throughout the day.

Tides are changeable but predictable (very much like my wife), and although you can positively guarantee there will be two high tides and two low tides each day, the times and heights will vary throughout each month. So just because one day you pitched up and dived into deep waters, you may find that the same spot at the same time the next day is just sand and seaweed. Great if you like building sandcastles, rubbish for DWS! And, even if you stay in one spot for the entire day, rising tides have a nasty habit of cutting off coves.

Fortunately, widely available surf forecasting websites and apps provide details of tide times and heights, weather and wave forecasts, and even include sea temperature - so now you have no excuse!

Whatever research you conduct on weather conditions, surf, and tides, still PHYSICALLY TAKE A LOOK at the water before you decide to climb.

How big and powerful are the waves?

Are there any obvious rip currents (i.e. strong currents which can drag you from the shoreline into deeper water)?

If the water is choppy or there are huge crashing waves, consider waiting, finding a safer spot, coming back another day, or maybe just trying a spot of crab fishing instead…

S... S... Scaling the heights - the S-scale grade system

Deep Water Soloing has developed a grade system over and above the sport climbing grade systems, but it's not about the level of difficulty: The S-scale/ grade is a measure of how SERIOUS climbing a route could be, even when you've got perfect weather, calm sea, deep water, and the ability to swim as well as a dolphin. My take on the grade descriptions are as follows:

S0 – SAFE SOLO

Lots of water (unless there's been a drought!), not too high, with easy exits out if you do happen to fall/jump in.

S1 – SO SO SOLO

There are some risks such as a higher climb or poor rock quality. Some areas of the climb may not be always directly above consistently deep water, so MOST DEFINITELY check the tides and take care of yourself!

S2 – SERIOUSLY SERIOUS SOLO

Likely to be seriously high, seriously hard, or seriously high and hard! And there may not be much water to land in if you haven't checked the tides correctly... and sometimes, even if you have checked the tides correctly! Attempting an S2 requires serious consideration.

S3 – SUICIDAL SOLO

The equivalent of free soloing over a thimble of water... shallow and extremely dangerous.

Ultimately you don't need to climb ridiculously high or difficult routes for DWS to be satisfying. Better to be in deep water than deep doo-doo!

Cold water shock

Like all outdoor climbing, the weather is going to be a significant influencing factor. And, even if the temperature on land is warm, the water you're climbing over won't necessarily be. For example, in the UK most DWS spots are found on the coastline, and when you consider that, for most of the year, the sea is only about 12 degrees, falling into the water mightn't be overly appealing.

Cold water shock is a very real phenomenon that can occur when someone jumps/falls into water below 15 degrees. Firstly, the sudden shock of unexpectedly entering cold water can cause your heart rate and breathing to suddenly increase. Secondly, when the cold water hits your skin the blood vessels constrict, making it harder for your heart to pump the blood around your body. Thirdly, an icy dip can literally 'take your breath away' (not in a pleasant, romantic way!), causing faster or potentially panicked breathing (Sad face). Throw into the mix, disorientation, soaked clothes and, perhaps even pain if you have fallen badly, and suddenly you could be in real danger (Really sad face)! Fortunately, there's a tried and tested remedy:

- Float onto your back.
- Try to relax.
- Keep calm (your body will soon acclimatise).
- Take a moment to catch your breath (it will return!).
- Call for help or swim back to safety.

The high dive

Falling safely

Ever been at the swimming pool when someone attempts a dive, but instead does a GIANT BELLY FLOP? The "CRACK" as they hit the surface of the water is louder than Indiana Jones' bull whip, and everyone goes "OOOOOOOOOooooooooooo!", waiting to see if the unfortunate will resurface without crying. There's a reason why professional divers enter the water in a clean straight line!

It's worth considering exactly how high you're going to climb. Remember our old pal GRAVITY? Well, when you fall, that old goat is going to pull you towards the water... at speed. The higher you climb the faster you're going to fall, and the faster you fall, the harder you will hit the water. For example, if I fell from 10 metres up, I'd travel at a speed of about 50 km/h. That's faster than the fastest man has ever run (Jamaican Sprinter Usain Bolt's top speed was 44.72km/h). What-is-more, you're going to go from MAXIMUM SPEED to almost ZERO in an instant. So HOW you hit the water is going be crucial.

Splayed out like a starfish
= BAD!

Feet first and straight as a pencil
= GOOD!

Let's be clear: in the same way as you could injure yourself following a bad fall on a bouldering mat, hitting the water in a funny (or not so funny) manner could cause similar bruising, sprains, or breaks. Practice jumps are a great way to gain confidence as well as accustom yourself to the water conditions.

Ideally, you want to minimise the surface area of your body that strikes the water, which might be easier said than done when you've got a second or two at most to react. Try and keep your back straight, your arms tightly by your sides, and your legs and feet together. You are aiming to stay rigid and as vertical as possible - there will be less stress on your body as you break the surface of the water. When you hit the water, keep your mouth closed and exhale through your nose. This should help prevent water going up your nose or into your mouth. There is certainly some literature suggesting that it may also be prudent to clench your buttocks as you enter the water. This is to prevent water from rushing in, a mystical yet dreaded affliction otherwise known as the SALTWATER ENEMA. I guess it's better to be safe than sorry!

Post DWS

Once you get back home, give your climbing shoes a wash in clean fresh water, otherwise the salt residue is going to make them look like they're covered in icing. If they're anything like the majority of climbing shoes in the world, they probably stink normally, but after soaking up a load of sea water they're going pong like a dead fish.

The least you need to know

- DWS is ill-advised if you can't swim.

- **When Deep Water Soloing it is essential that you consider additional hazards such as rocks beneath the surface, the temperature of the water, tides, wave height, rip currents, and the depth of the water over which you will be climbing.**

- **A commonly used grade system for Deep Water Soloing is the S-scale, a measure of how serious climbing a route above water can be, and ranges from S0-S3.**

- **When falling or jumping, try to hit the water in a clean vertical straight line.**

- **DWS sounds serious… and it is (particularly an S3!), but when done with foreplanning and caution it can be one of the most exciting ways to experience climbing.**

13

IT AIN'T JUST BRAWN, KNUCKLEHEAD! INTELLIGENT TRAINING

The movies are full of examples of the underdog rising to an impossible challenge, doing a short period of intense exercise and overnight becoming faster, stronger, or fitter - from 'average Joe' to accomplished boxer, kung-fu artist, or champion of the universe. But, if it was that easy, everyone would be doing it... And there'd probably be an app!

You will always be able to improve at climbing, but like most things in life, there is no quick fix. Improvement requires dedication and perseverance. Focused training will help create a 'virtuous circle' (not to be confused with a 'vicious circle' which is a whole different ball game!), whereby the POSITIVE PAYBACK from your action helps motivate you to continue the process.

This chapter will help you to maximise your potential by training in the key focus areas of:

- Technique.
- Strength.
- Flexibility.
- Mindset.

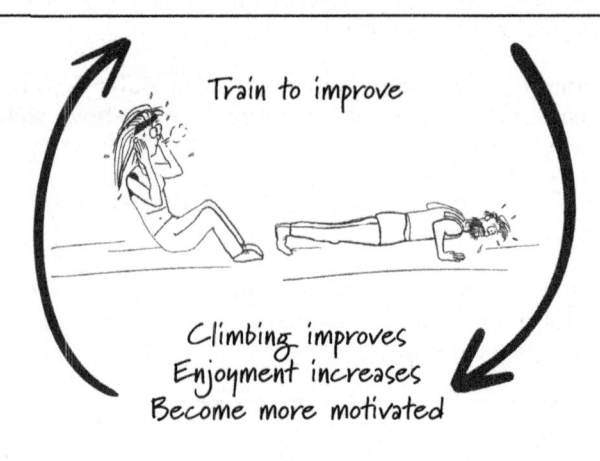

Train to improve

*Climbing improves
Enjoyment increases
Become more motivated*

Technique

Practice, practice, practice...

Knowing the existence of the different techniques and moves described in this book is Stage 1 in your climbing journey. Stage 2 requires you putting theory into PRACTICE, PRACTICE, and yet more PRACTICE. When you start any new skill, it takes conscious thought to execute it correctly. So, when attempting your first drop knee for example, you might really have to concentrate on each stage of the move:

1. *Gripping the hold with straight arms.*
2. *Moving your foot high on a hold.*
3. *Dropping your knee into position.*
4. *Swinging your hips towards the wall.*
5. *Reaching up for the next hold.*

If you repeatedly practice the move, this will help the transition from your conscious mind, where you're thinking about how to do it, to your subconscious mind, where it becomes second nature. You just 'know' how to do it.

Whilst the techniques required to ascend a route will be broadly similar, every climb is different, requiring an infinite number of variations of each move. One thing is abundantly clear: if you want to improve your climbing, you need to climb as much as possible.

The more you physically climb, the better you will come to understand the strength and limitations of your own body, as well as developing intuitive understanding of what moves work in any given scenario.

"Yeah, in today's 'sess' I'm going to practice an infinite number of variations of each move ... reckon I'll be finished by the end of time as we know it..."

Exactly WHAT to practice, practice, practice...

There are numerous climbing exercises that you can perform, that specifically target different aspects of technique, and practising them will add a little bit more structure to your training. These are my favourite:

Silent feet

"Ssssssssssssssssssssssssssssssh… listen…"

Each poorly positioned or unnecessary foot placement results in energy expenditure. 'Silent feet' is a useful exercise for developing awareness of precise foot placement. Stepping on the best part of a hold with the correct part of your foot allows for better stability, balance, and efficiency of movement. The concept is simple: make as little noise as possible when stepping between holds. If your feet are scraping and clumping around like Frankenstein's monster, then it's a fair bet you need to improve your footwork!

Noise is your enemy. The only way to conquer this challenge is learning to precisely place your foot on each hold and move smoothly between them. Alternatively, learn to climb with cotton wool on the bottom of your shoes.

Sticky feet

When I say, "sticky feet", I'm not encouraging the use of glue as a means of improving your climbing. Many climbers have a crisis of indecision when they're attempting a route. They'll move their foot to one hold and then reconsider their move and move it back, perhaps moving their other foot there and swapping it around - again and again, back and forth - like they're doing a savage version of the tango! By the time they reach the top of the climb they could have climbed it 5 times over already.

Sticky feet is another exercise to help improve the precision of your footwork, focusing on making the best foot placement every time. When you climb with sticky feet, imagine that the moment you place your foot on a hold it's instantly glued in place. There's no shuffling around, edging left or right, or swapping feet. Once it's there, it's a STUCK FOOT! Now clearly this exercise would be (a) short-lived and (b) incredibly annoying to you and anyone else wanting to climb the route if your foot remained stuck on the first hold you touched! As such, you can continue moving up the climb, sticking to each new foothold as you go…

You may have figured out already that this exercise can also be undertaken in combination with those other useful climbing appendages… I'm talking about

STICKY HANDS (Yikes, what were you thinking!). Practising sticky hands will help you hone your focus on how to best grip a hold, so that rather than just grabbing it any-old-how, you seek to position your fingers and hand in the most secure and beneficial position to aid your ascent.

Straight arms

Honestly, I couldn't think of a catchy title for this exercise, but climbing with straight arms is essential. It ensures that your body weight hangs off your skeleton, rather than relying on the inefficient muscular requirements of bent arms. It's easy to lapse between the two, so having a concentrated session of rigidly straight-armed climbing will help you become less reliant on PULLING with your arms, and rather, ascending by moving your lower body and PUSHING with your legs.

You can practice, either by paying strict attention to your arm position, or asking a friend to call out whenever you bend your arms. This is best practised on a route that genuinely lends itself to sustained straight-armed climbing, such as a gentle overhang with good hand holds. Consider placing tape around your elbows to slightly restrict movement, but not so much that you can't move them or cut off your blood supply! (I did toy with the idea of strapping broomsticks to my arms, but apart from looking like an absolute lunatic, the chances of injury were exceedingly high, and besides, who has two broomsticks?!).

Blindfolded climbing

Whilst not recommended over a pool of crocodiles, climbing blindfolded under controlled conditions (i.e. on a top rope or traversing a boulder with a super-focused spotter) can help you develop greater awareness of your body; particularly your balance and the effect of position on your stability. We heavily rely on our sight and removing this key sense forces you to consider other variants. So, rather than looking at a foothold and developing an opinion of what it is like, you must step on it and FEEL its potential.

Down-climbing

When you're walking around, normally you look in the direction you are going. So, when you climb down a route, looking down should come naturally. But as it happens, climbing downwards can feel very unnatural (particularly after all that UP climbing). Down-climbing really helps you improve your footwork because it gets you to focus on your feet, rather than your hands. After you've successfully climbed up to the top of a route, down-climbing presents as a great opportunity for footwork practice.

Plus 1

'Plus 1' is a fun and sociable way to train endurance on the wall and tests a climber's ability to move on an incredibly fluid route. Played with two or more participants, it simply involves each player (climber) picking which hold to use next in sequence. Once a player has climbed the made-up route, they add a new hold, and the process starts again. It's easy at the start, but as more holds are added (a new one each time a participant finishes the route), the harder it becomes. It can be as easy or difficult as you like and tailored to match your specific needs, such as creating longer routes for stamina, or only using specific holds (e.g. slopers).

Strength

There is no getting away from it, strength is important to climbing and, whilst you don't need to be able to bench press a rhino or do one finger pull ups to make significant progress (despite what some online 'experts' might suggest), it makes perfect sense to spend time developing the specific muscle groups used in climbing.

Like any sport, sustained workouts of one muscle group will lead to the body adapting to its environment. So, although climbing uses a wide variety of muscles, it's worth mentioning that if, for example, you just focus your climbing on steep overhanging routes, your back and shoulder muscles are likely to become over-developed. You want to avoid the so-called 'climbers' posture' (rounded upper back and shoulders as well as an underdeveloped chest), and reduce the likelihood of injury from muscle imbalance, by ensuring you engage in a well rounded exercise program.

"I really think you should concentrate on exercising other muscle groups..."

I fully understand doing strength training exercises instead of climbing mightn't be a particularly appetising prospect, but... and it's a BIG BUT (just to clarify – not a BIG BUTT through sustained exercising of your glutes), if you can motivate yourself to do so, your body will become stronger, ultimately enabling you to climb harder and longer.

I have listed a few basic strength exercises that can be completed at any point, before or after climbing, and without the need for additional exercise equipment (so you literally have no excuse for doing them). I haven't specified how many reps you should do of each exercise because that will vary hugely depending on your level of fitness. But usually, doing 1-3 sets in multiples of 5 or 10 is a good place to begin.

There is one obvious area that I have not included, and that is finger strengthening exercises. Strong fingers are crucial in developing as a climber. Many climbing gyms come with a variety of 'hang boards' (you guessed it – boards to hang on) and other apparatus specifically targeting finger strength, mainly through sustained hanging (with or without weights). Whilst there can be definite benefits to such training, fingers are delicate structures, and certainly in the earlier stages of one's climbing career, the best way to strengthen your fingers is to climb. My best advice would be to get an assessment from a qualified coach before you engage in finger specific strength training.

So, starting from the…

TOP (Upper body)

1. Press-ups

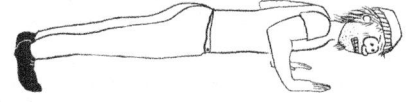

You knew it was coming didn't you. I mean, doesn't literally every exercise program include press-ups? The point in doing them, is that they will help you counterbalance all the PULLING you are doing climbing, by PUSHING instead.

- Keep your back straight and your arms shoulder width apart.
- Tighten your core (suck your belly button in).
- Keep your legs straight and balance on your toes.
- Keeping your forearms vertical, bend your arms and press your body directly downwards so that your chest nearly touches the floor.
- Push back up again.
- Keep your elbows in throughout the exercise.

You can make this easier by resting your knees on the ground. You can make it even easier by not doing the press-ups at all! Press-ups are surprisingly diverse. Not a statement you hear every day! By altering position slightly, you can concentrate the workout on different muscles. So, with wider arms you can focus on your chest muscles, with hands closer together you can focus on your triceps, and one arm forwards and one backwards (staggered) increases stress on the opposing arm… the list of exhausting press-up variants is endless! Enjoy!

2. Pull-ups

For most, pull-ups aren't something you just crack on and do. So, at first, you mightn't be able to do any at all! But, as we know, climbing involves a lot of pulling so it makes sense to focus on the muscles involved in the pull! With all exercise, 'form' is EVERYTHING… to avoid injury and ensure that you are working ALL of the right muscles correctly. Ideally you want to do the pull-up on a bespoke pull-up bar, but you can conceivably do them off any available ledge.

- With straightened arms, reach overhead, gripping slightly wider than your shoulders.
- Your hands should be facing away from you.
- Keep your feet together and point your toes.
- Tighten your core.
- Pull down with your elbows.
- Pull until you chin is over the bar (or ledge) and hold momentarily.
- Lower (rather than drop) yourself down to the straight-armed position.
- Keep your neck and chin in a neutral position throughout.

If you can't pull yourself all the way up and down, there are a few things you can do to work your way there: Hang in the straight-armed position and pull your shoulders downwards and then back to the start position repeatedly. This will help you gain the strength to be able to start the pull-up. You can also try pull-ups with your feet on a box, chair, or a really understanding buddy so that you get used to the required body position and movement, without the strain of pulling your entire body weight. Make the pull-up harder by lessening the amount of assistance provided by your legs (e.g. use one leg to support your body).

3. I –Y - T

I-Y-T exercises target the rhomboids and trapezius – the muscles in your back (not to be confused with a diamond shaped quadrilateral or a parallelogram with adjacent sides that are unequal lengths).

I

- Lay on your front with your arms straight in the I position.
- Tighten your core, glutes (butt to you and me), and legs (you should know what they are).
- Lift your arms up as if you are trying to squeeze your shoulder blades *up and together*.
- Repeat.

Y

- Lay on your front with your arms in the Y position.
- Tighten your core, glutes, and legs.
- Lift your arms up as if you are trying to squeeze your shoulder blades *back and down*.
- Repeat.

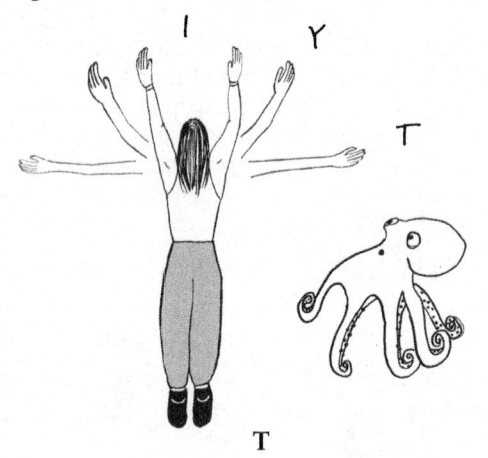

T

- Lay on your front with your arms straight in the… yeah, you guessed it, the T position.
- Tighten your core, glutes, and legs.
- Lift your arms up as if you are trying to squeeze your shoulder blades *together*.
- Repeat.

MIDDLE (core)

You will be forgiven for wondering what a strong core has to do with climbing. I mean, you pull with your arms and push with your legs – what the heck has the bit in the middle got to do, except come along for the ride, heh? Well, fact is, it's your core that creates the tension in your body that can keep you locked into position close to the wall, enabling you to statically reach for a high hold, stick a dyno, or glue your feet to the holds on a steep section of wall.

"Work on your core you Nana!"

4. **Plank (the exercise, not you!)**

- Start on all fours.
- Place your forearms on the floor parallel to one another.
- Your elbows should be under your shoulders.
- Tense your stomach and raise your knees so that you are balancing on your toes.
- Keep your body straight.
- Look at the ground between your hands.
- Hold position for 1 minute.
- Mumble frustratedly to yourself as time itself seems to slow down…

5. **Side plank (Yeah – take a wild guess…)**

- Lie on your side with your legs stacked one on top of the other.
- Keep your upper arm straight along your side.
- Bend your lower arm so that it is at a 90-degree angle.
- Your elbow should be under your shoulder.
- Raise your hips off the ground as you push down on your lower arm.
- Maintain a straight body.
- Hold position and then change sides.

Your core may well shake and wobble with the strain, which is fine, but try not to dip your hips or place excessive strain on your shoulder.

This exercise is also good for shoulder stabilisation.

6. **Super-man/woman (Wearing a cape is obligatory)**

- Start in the press up position, with your back straight, and your arms and legs shoulder width apart.
- Raise your right arm straight in front of you, whilst at the same time raising your left leg straight behind you.
- Hold for (e.g.) 10 seconds and swap.

Avoid Kryptonite whilst practising

Feel like you are flying?

No... Well you do need to have a seriously good imagination... And if flying works your core as much as this exercise, I wouldn't fly very often even if I could. This is a tough exercise which is good for strengthening the core, back, and shoulders.

BOTTOM

Finally, remember those massive muscles beneath your waist that are responsible for literally driving you up the wall? Leg exercises are equally important for stabilisation and power:

7. **Squats**

- Stand with your feet slightly wider than shoulder width.
- Feet should be at 45-degree angles (that's outwards, not inwards!).
- Keeping your back straight throughout, bend your knees.
- Lower yourself into a seated position (minus the seat).
- Hold your arms straight out in front of you if it helps to maintain balance.
- Squeeze your buttocks and stand up.
- Repeat.

8. **Lateral (side) squats**

- Stand with your legs wide apart.
- Feet should be facing forward (throughout the exercise).
- Keeping your back straight and chest up, bend one knee and sit backwards (into an invisible chair).
- Your other leg should be kept completely straight.
- Keep both feet flat on the floor.
- Stand back up to centre and repeat on the other leg.
- Keep your core engaged throughout.
- Repeat.

The strength to continue

You can always supplement the outlined exercises with your own. Go onto the web or social media and inevitably there is an A-S-T-R-O-N-O-M-I-C-A-L amount of information on different exercises that will make you leaner, stronger, faster, healthier, happier, etc... You could spend a few minutes, hours, days, or weeks sifting through the material, searching for that perfect workout. If you're anything like me, you'll probably disappear off on several tangents – reading about a man who lifts weights with his ears, videos of a crocodile eating a lion or vice versa, or sifting pictures of a cute puppy (Awwwwwwwww!) ...BACK IN THE ROOM PEOPLE, BACK IN THE ROOM!

Basically, research is great, but try and focus your searches specifically to "training for rock climbing". Doing an 8-week program to get yourself a "super toned butt" may look nice, but it's not going to help you climb. Also, check that whoever is providing the workout has some credibility (having lots of INSTAGRAM followers doesn't necessarily count). And recognise your own limitations: you are unlikely to benefit from an outrageously long and strenuous workout that is aimed at elite climbers. I'm not saying you might not need it one day, but find the right balance for you... and stick to it!

Personally, I would AVOID any sites/apps sporting outrageously muscular beefcakes / super toned super models preening and posing. It has taken a lot of make-up, great editing, and obscene personal sacrifice to look like that in front of the camera. If you look at pictures/videos of REAL climbers, you will soon come to realise that YOU DON'T HAVE TO LOOK LIKE A SUPERHUMAN TO CLIMB LIKE ONE. The key to maintaining or improving your strength is being consistent in your training. Recognising that I've probably missed my opportunity to go to the Olympics by about 30 years, I just train a couple of hours a week, concentrating on the weaker parts of my body (...okay, yeah, pretty much all of it these days!), so that it can physically cope with the demands placed upon it.

If the idea of committing yourself to a concentrated period of strength exercises fills you full of dread, then think about ways to add a little workout into your daily routine instead. For example, standing on one leg every time you brush your teeth will help increase your leg and ankle stability. If you're off to get groceries, walk the distance rather than drive, using your shopping bags as improvised weights: roll your shoulders, raise, and lower the bags to the sides and front, or straighten and curl your fingers. Squat each time you unload an item into your cupboard. Even when you're just slouched in front of the TV, there's no excuse. Simply squeezing a tennis ball, or stretching an elastic band wrapped around your fingers, will target the muscles in your hands and forearms that move your fingers (fingers don't have muscles... who knew?!), which are so crucial to climbing. Any effort, however small, will eventually lead to increments in strength. Bottom line is, even doing a little bit here and there is better than doing nothing at all!

Flexibility

Ironically, whilst many motivated climbers dedicate time trying to improve their strength, they often ignore an equally important element – flexibility. It's no good being a giant throbbing lump of muscle, if you can barely raise your arms over your head. I'm neither a throbbing lump of muscle, nor flexible, which is doubly annoying. When I was a youngster (once upon a time, many years ago), I competed in cross country events, running for miles. But once I was over the finish line, I'd be straight off home for tea in front of the TV. I don't remember stretching my muscles after exercise until I was about 30, which is probably why I can wave at my toes but can't touch them. When you undertake any vigorous exercise, your muscles contract, and you need to help them get back to their normal length by a consistent program of stretching.

Now, I'm not saying you need to be able to pull your legs around your head (although they would make for a good party trick), and I do realise stretching at the end of a climbing session can be a bit of a pain in the butt (particularly a glute stretch). However, stretching will relieve tight muscles and tendons, reduce tension, and help maintain flexibility. So, on balance, stretching is pretty handy! But, it is important to stretch correctly.

These are some essential Stretching Do's and Don'ts:

DO

- Relax – it is not meant to be a battle between you and your body!

- Focus on the muscles you are stretching.

- Breathe into the area you are stretching.

- Use the stretching time as a period to slowly unwind.

DON'T

- Hold your breath.

- Bounce or jolt your body – it will initiate the 'stretch reflex' causing your muscles to tighten!

- Stretch to the point of pain - you are now overstretching!

I've been in group stretching sessions where someone has displayed levels of flexibility that I'd normally associate with a bizarre circus act. There may be a temptation to try and push your body to match others. DON'T! Think of a big box of different sized elastic bands: thick ones, thin ones, long ones, short ones... Like muscles, they are all going to have different levels of strength and stretch. Pushing too hard could cause injury, like a muscle tear and, to continue the comparison, a snapped elastic band is no good to anyone!

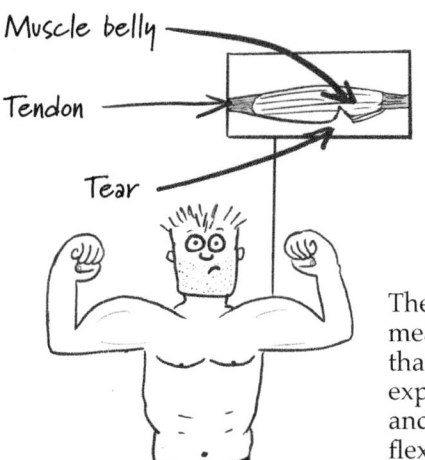

Muscle belly
Tendon
Tear

Rubber bands 300g

"I should have stretched more!"

They say, "Rome wasn't built in a day". I mean... Obvs! Well, equally obvs is the fact that you can't stretch for one day and then expect to do the splits. Only consistent and targeted stretching will lead to better flexibility.

So, if doing the splits is your goal, it will be achievable if you dedicate time and energy to your stretching. Eitherway, the more flexibility you achieve, the better range of movement your limbs will have, and the easier it will be for you to move through challenging routes. I've compiled some basic warm-down stretches to be completed post climbing. These will help maintain your flexibility. They can also be undertaken practically anytime, anyplace, anywhere because, if you really want to improve your flexibility, then you need to think about developing a habit of stretching every day.

1. **Forearm & wrist stretch**

Start in the 'tabletop position' with your arms directly below your shoulders and knees below your hips.

Turn your hands so that your fingers are pointing towards your body. Keep your palms flat on the ground and gently lean backwards until you feel the stretch. Hold for at least 30 seconds.

Be careful not to lock your elbows. Some people have hyperflexible elbows which, although a seemingly fab party trick, is not good for your joints. So, keep your arms slightly bent.

Now turn your hands over so that the backs of your hands lay flat on the ground. Gently lean backwards until you feel the stretch in your forearms. Hold for at least 30 seconds.

2. **Lat stretch**

Otherwise known as the latissimus dorsi muscles, 'lats' provide shoulder and back stability and strength, so important in climbing:

Kneel, and then reach your arms out in front of you. Lower your body to the ground with your thumbs facing up, your arms straight, and your forehead resting gently on the ground. Pull your arms back and push your palms down until you feel the stretch in your shoulders.

To vary the stretch, you can widen your legs, or just have one arm forward and the other at your side. Most people are tighter on one side than the other, so it's also good to walk your fingers in one direction until you feel the stretch. Then repeat on the other side. You may look like you're doing a bizarre version of 'Incy Wincy Spider', but if it feels good, keep going! Hold for at least 30 seconds.

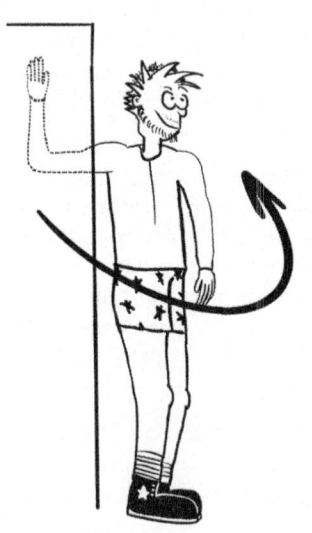

3. **Chest stretch**

You need a wall, doorway, or solid structure to lean on for this stretch, which focuses on relieving TIGHT PECS!

Raise your arm with your elbow bent to form the perfect 90 angle. Standing sideways on, place your forearm on whatever solid structure you have chosen to aid the stretch. Gently ease your body forwards until you feel a stretch across your upper chest. Hold for at least 30 seconds before changing arms.

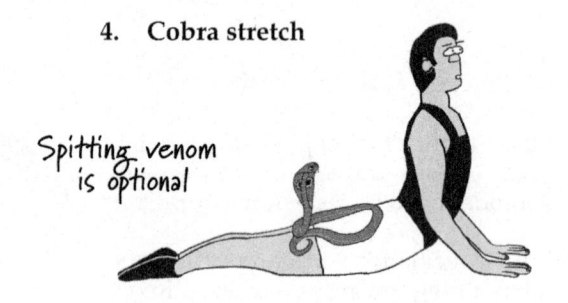

4. **Cobra stretch**

Spitting venom is optional

I guess 'cobra stretch' sounds better than 'back and stomach stretch', and you'll be relieved to know, there's no need to rise slowly out of a basket to the haunting tunes of a snake charmer's mystic flute:

Lying face down with your elbows bent and by your side, place the palms of your hands on the ground. Push your upper body upright, straightening your arms. Keep your breathing steady and do not lock your elbows.

Hold for at least 30 seconds.

5. Groin stretch

Sit on the floor. Bend your legs and put the soles of your feet together. Hold onto your feet and, bending from the hips, lean your upper body forward. You can also push your elbows down onto your knees to increase the stretch.

Hold for at least 30 seconds.

You will quickly determine whether you need to work at this stretch - high knees in the sitting position are an indication of tight muscles.

6. Hip flexors stretch

If you sit down for long periods you'll likely have tight hip flexors, as they shorten over time. This is of no use whatsoever if you want the ability to stretch out to footholds or step high climbing a route.

Kneel on one knee. Your front leg should be at 90-degrees with your foot flat on the floor. Your back leg should be stretched out behind, and your body upright.

Rest your hands on your front leg or, for a deeper stretch, raise them straight in the air. Squeeze your bum to 'lock your hips' in place and, keeping your back straight and your core tight, ease your hips forward.

Hold for at least 30 seconds. And then, swap legs.

7. Leg stretch

Sit on the floor with one leg straight. Bend the other leg so the sole of your foot touches the inside of your thigh (No, that's not the stretching bit yet).

Leaning from the hips, slide your hands down your straight leg until you feel a stretch at the back of your leg (hamstrings and calves).

Keep your foot at 90 degrees and hold for at least 30 seconds.

Swap legs and repeat.

8. **Frog stretch**

Frog stretch is a groin and hip stretch double whammy! But it can feel intense, if not a little unpleasant, so gently does it:

Assume the tabletop position. Keeping your arms shoulder width apart and your palms face down, lower yourself on to your forearms. Flex your ankles and turn your feet out, so that your inner ankles touch the floor. Slowly move your knees out to the sides so that your inner knees touch the floor (the wider you move your knees, the greater the stretch… so move SLOWLY!!!).

Hold for at least… you've guessed it… 30 seconds. Reverse out of it.

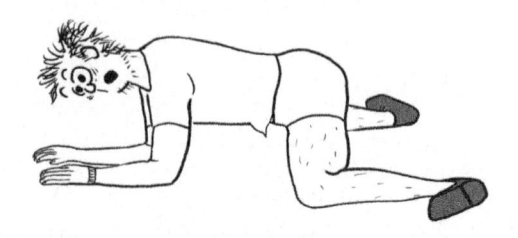

I would suggest you ensure your butt is facing a wall when doing this stretch, otherwise you're likely to give the local vicar a heart attack!

9. **Whole body**

Lay on your back. Reach your straightened arms overhead. Straighten your legs and point your toes. Imagine you are on a medieval rack and stretch in opposite directions (ideally without tearing yourself in two, unlike a medieval rack).

Hold for a few seconds and repeat…Satisfaction guaranteed!

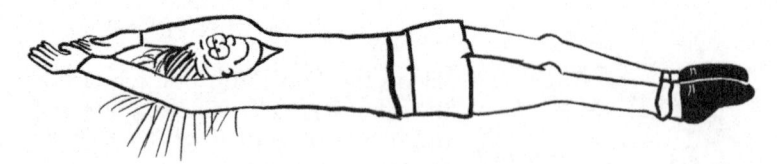

Rest for a minute or two on your back and just breathe easy. Close your eyes, catch some flies… just chill. You've earned it.

Mindset

We've established that to become a great climber you need to (a) concentrate on your technique and climb a lot, (b) do climbing specific strength training, and (c) focus on improving your flexibility. And yet you could still fail to reach your full potential. Why? Because even with the strongest, fittest, and most flexible body, if you don't have the right mindset, you are likely to underachieve.

Climbing can be MENTALLY DEMANDING. At a time when you may be pushing your body to the limit, immense concentration is required in applying technical knowledge to complex situations. Add to this the expectations you might put on yourself to perform, worries of failure, or the fear of falling and it's understandable that, even if you're physically perfect, you might not be mentally equipped to deal with the pressure effectively. Here are some areas upon which to focus that will help you cope with the mental challenges that climbing can bring:

i. Mind over matter… If you don't mind, it doesn't matter

Having the right mindset is imperative. Whilst highly sociable, climbing is also a very personal experience. When it comes down to brass tacks, it's only you who can decide what your next move will be, how to execute it, and how far you want to comfortably go. Anything but positivity will hinder your ability to achieve your goals.

If you are climbing with friends, they will no doubt provide encouragement. And encouragement can boost your performance. Don't we always tend to try harder when others are egging us on? If those same friends started saying, "You're never going to do it," or "That's too difficult for you," then it would be demotivating and probably upsetting… And time to get some new friends!!!

It's the same with your inner self-talk. If you say to yourself, "That looks too hard…", "I'm not good enough…", and, "I can't…", then it will also negatively affect your performance. You fall on a climb and your negative mindset will be going, "Meh, told you, you couldn't do it… you're soooo rubbish!" Failure becomes a self-fulfilling prophecy.

It's important to RECOGNISE negative or unhelpful thoughts.

Once you've identified them, REPLACE THEM!

"I'm never going to be able to climb 'the Spout', it's 6B+…"

REPLACE:

"I'll never be able to climb that..." with, **"I can learn to climb that."**

"I'm not strong enough to do that climb..." with, **"I'll get strong enough to do that climb."**

"This route is impossible..." with, **"I can work on how to do this route."**

More than you'll realise, the difference between achieving an ascent or not, is just confidence in your own ability. Often, climbers will look at route and say, "NO WAY is that possible!" Then some random dude will come along and ascend it... What do you realise? The route is achievable after all.

There are always two ways of looking at a difficult climbing problem: CHALLENGE or IMPOSSIBILITY.

Focus on the challenge of solving the problem, rather than making a judgement on your ability to perform.

The RIGHT frame of mind kicks impossibility in the ass and tells it to, "Go take a hike..." (Or words to that effect).

ii.   **FEAR of falling...**

I remember when I first started climbing, the higher I got, the more nervous I became. It was bad enough bouldering, but when I tried rope climbing for the first time, the feeling was magnified. A few metres up and my hands had become super sweaty (nothing like trying to hold on when your mitts are all wet). And, as my grip felt less secure, I grasped the holds harder... and harder... so that by the time I reached the top of the climb I was exhausted, and my forearms were ready to BURST. As the belayer began lowering me to the ground, I started to relax, and suddenly realised I'd been holding my breath for most of the climb! Like the pigeon-chasing dog (Chapter 5), I had got totally caught up in the moment. So, there I was: light-headed, gasping for breath, sweating profusely, shaking with anxiety, with searing pain down my arms...

Symptoms of a heart attack:

Feeling light-headed or dizzy
Shortness of breath
Profuse sweating
Overwhelming feeling of anxiety
Pain in the arm and / or chest

Fortunately, I wasn't having a heart attack (and I didn't know what the symptoms were back then anyway... so even if I was having one, I wouldn't have realised it... even luckier I wasn't having one eh?!). I had just got myself REALLY worked up about falling.

False Evidence Appearing Real

The FEAR of falling can be crippling. But just as I said in Chapter 3, "worry, anxiety, and even nasty, butterfly-inducing, squeaky bottom fear is completely and utterly normal." Those unpleasant feelings are completely natural. A healthy body feels the effects of adrenaline when faced with danger, preparing for 'fight' or 'flight'. But contrary to what your body is telling you, you are NOT in any danger. If you fall whilst bouldering, you're going to land on soft matting. If you fall whilst rope climbing, you're going to be caught and held in the air by the belayer. You're NOT going to suffer a serious injury or die (It wouldn't be a popular sport if that was the general consequence)! These symptoms, caused by adrenaline, cannot hurt you either. Simply recognising and accepting this fact will help.

Face Everything And Recover

Here's something you don't often get in a climbing manual – a Shakespeare quote: "Present fears are less than horrible imaginings," which I roughly translate as, "Dude, it's not as bad as you think it is!"

Psychological research has established that, if you stay in a position you fear – like clambering up the edge of a boulder or dangling high in the air on the end of a rope - your anxiety will go up, plateau, and then go down again. The more times you place yourself in the same situation, your anxiety will be less severe, and those nasty feelings will dissipate more quickly. It's a process of SYSTEMATIC DESENSITISATION, a technique that is used to help people overcome phobias. So, if climbing and/or fearing falling causes anxiety, then it actually pays to FEEL THE FEAR AND DO IT ANYWAY.

Of course, you don't have to wait until your next fall. You can practice falling. This works particularly well with rope climbing because you can climb as high as you dare and, at a prearranged moment with your belayer, just drop. As much as your instinct might be to quickly try and scramble back onto the wall (clamped back on to those reassuring holds), I would encourage you to just hold on a sec:

In that moment, hanging in the air, let the anxiety take its grip. Okay, so it's not going to be a pleasant feeling, but it can't harm you in any way... it's just a feeling! Get your feet on the wall, your legs slightly bent and shoulder width apart, and your arms by your side. Just take a minute to regain your composure and have a look around... you're likely to have the best view in the house! Concentrate on your breathing. Take nice deep, slow breaths, and shake your arms out, relieving some of the tension in your body. Just hang there for a while (let your belayer know that's your intention beforehand!). Appreciate that you are high up and yet completely safe. And then, only when you are ready, get back on the wall.

Have confidence in the knowledge that, every time you do this, anxiety is going to be there, but its hold on you will get weaker, and weaker, and weaker.

(Whenever I feel the familiar sickly feeling of anxiety washing over me, I also utilise my own somewhat unscientific coping strategy by gently whispering, "Kiss my butt anxiety!" You're unlikely to find that suggestion in a psychology book, but it works for me).

Remember to BREATHE!

You will recall from Chapter 5, some of the physiological benefits of breathing correctly whilst climbing. Concentrating specifically on your breathing can also help move the focus away from your inner worries. Sometimes, it's difficult to get over the unpleasant feelings gnawing at your stomach, but one technique that is proven to help keep you calm when under pressure is BOX BREATHING. It is so powerful, it is reportedly used by U.S. NAVY SEALS (just to be clear, I mean the elite special forces unit... not cute, American marine animals). I have been entrusted to provide you with this highly secret tactic, which as you would expect, is available to read about all over the internet... But, since you're here, sit down with your feet flat on the floor OR lie down:

STEP 1:

Inhale (slowly and steadily) for 4 seconds

STEP 4

Hold your breath for 4 seconds

REPEAT

STEP 2:

Hold your breath for 4 seconds

STEP 3

Exhale (slowly and steadily) for 4 seconds

As you can see, it's a very straight forward process, and is just one of several anxiety reducing breathing exercises that might just help push back those nerves. I've added an optional extra:

STEP 5:

Shout:
"Climbing gym ATTTENNNNN-SHUN!
Commence.... BREATHING!"
at the top of your voice.

Although it is unlikely to help your anxiety, breathing technique, climbing ability, or chances of getting into the US Navy Seals.

(iii) Three things

Often, our brains fixate on what went wrong. You might remember a bad fall or a climb you felt embarrassed that you couldn't do. When we think negative thoughts, we also experience the associated negative feelings. To combat this, it's important to celebrate your achievements and feed off the positive feelings that come with it. A great way of doing this is by keeping a record. Every time you go climbing write down three POSITIVE things about your day. For example:

- *Climbed today with lots of energy...*
- *Had a laugh at a hold shaped like a phallus...*
- *Got to eat a cookie as big as my head after a good training session...*

Diarising THREE THINGS is a fabulous way of reminding yourself of your POSITIVE experiences and achievements. This will help you focus on the things that were good about your climbing experience and the accompanying positive feelings.

Besides, everyone who starts rock climbing, other than maybe a baby gorilla, begins with a degree of trepidation: grips too hard, pulls too much with their arms, worries unnecessarily about falling, and may as well have been wearing wellington boots for the utter lack of precision in footwork. Documenting this journey will help you realise just how far you have come.

(iv) Visualisation

Visualisation is a technique employed by a significant number of professional athletes to help better prepare and focus their mind on the task ahead. It's based on the concept that your brain has difficultly deciphering the difference between reality and imagination. So, in theory, if you imagine yourself climbing a difficult route, this could help you climb it for real. If you've raised your eyebrows (or imagined you've raised your eyebrows) at this idea, you need to understand there is a HUGE body of supporting scientific evidence suggesting that visualisation can have positive effects on performance, motivation, endurance, pain management, and self-confidence. What this doesn't mean is that you can lay back, chill out, think of climbing something tough for 20 minutes and then you're going to be an amazing climber. No, no, no, no noooooooooo... But it is an additional tool in your toolbox which might just positively impact how you think about, feel, and execute a climb.

Visualisation practice is about thinking and feeling EXACTLY what it will be like to climb a route.

You are essentially mentally rehearsing your performance on a route, so you want to try and imagine every single aspect of the climb, from the moment you approach the route, to getting to the top.

It's important to try and reinforce positive images (e.g. you ascending the route), rather than letting negative self-chatter get the better of you.

"I visualised myself falling off and... I fell off... spooky heh?!"

So, before you climb a difficult route, study it, and then sit back, close your eyes if it helps, and relax. Try and clear your mind of everything else and just concentrate on imagining how it would feel to climb it. Consider factors, such as:

- The feeling of each hold against your skin.
- The position of your body in relation to the wall.
- The sound of your breathing.
- The angle of your hand as you grip each hold.
- The exertion required to make each move.

Work your way up that route in your mind and feel the sense of achievement when you reach the last hold. Once you've mentally smashed it, give it a go for real!

Visualisation is a skill, requiring dedication and practice, but the better you are at visualisation, the greater the benefits felt.

Reviewing your progress in the 4 focus areas

If you've ever played a computer game, you'll know that they often involve choosing between characters who have different skill levels. When I was a kid (back when time began) I used to play a dungeons and dragons arcade game which involved four characters, each of whom had different strengths and weaknesses: one was crazy strong, destroying any nasties that got too close to him, another had amazing firepower, obliterating every monster in the room. The third, armoured character, could survive sustained attacks and the final character was lightning fast, speeding around the screen whilst the others lumbered behind.

So... at this point you may be thinking, "Well this is all very interesting (NOT!), but will it help my climbing?"

The answer is, "Nope!" What I do think is helpful though, is thinking about your own strengths and weaknesses in the same simplistic terms. Climbing requires the right combination of TECHNIQUE, STRENGTH, FLEXIBILITY, and MINDSET.

If you were a computer game character, where the aim of the game is to ascend climbs of increasing difficulty, consider rating yourself on a scale of 1-10. My character, 'The Ambitious One', would have the following ratings:

Low skill rating------------------------------------High skill rating
1   10
                    Technique
                                          Strength
                        Flexibility
                                                    Mindset

My character has got a very positive mindset but seriously needs to work on technique (or find a MAGIC POTION)! Be honest with yourself and think, "Where am I now with my climbing?" and, "Where do I want to be?" If you can only manage ½ a press-up and lifting a ripe melon is too much for you, then can you really score yourself 9 out of 10 for strength? But if you can get both legs around your ears then you can probably score flexibility quite high!

Record your profile as you see yourself NOW and then review it in a few months. This can be as scientifically based as you wish... or not. For example, if you are super keen on ascertaining your strength, you could enlist the help of a gym instructor, or simply make a record of how many press-ups, pull-ups, or squats you can do in a minute. Compare results a week later, a month later, and 3 months later. If you find you have improved in one area but not in another, set yourself a new focus area challenge.

In summary, if you want to get better at climbing, then invest as much time and energy on your WEAKNESSES as you do your strengths. By targeting the areas you are not so good at, you will see a greater overall improvement. Also, recognise that every effort you make to pursue your goal will get you a step closer to achieving it. How big a step is determined by how much effort you are willing to make.

The least you need to know

- **Practising different climbing moves and techniques will promote the transition from your conscious mind, where you're thinking about how to do it, to your subconscious mind, where it becomes second nature.**

- **Climbing is a sport requiring a balanced training approach to reduce the likelihood of muscle imbalance.**

- **Stretching will relieve tight muscles and tendons, reduce tension, help maintain flexibility, and improve recovery time.**

- **Focus on the problem at hand rather than your own performance, accept that sometimes you will feel anxious, and celebrate the positives.**

14

CLIMBING IS NOT A COMPETITION... UNLESS IT IS A COMPETITION

Going to a competition can be a very exciting and fun way of testing your skills against others. Sounds okay... heh? Fancy taking the plunge (I mean into the competition world... not OFF the wall)?!

This chapter provides competition hints and tips that will help you make the step with confidence, including:

- What to pack in advance.
- How to prepare.
- On the day do's and don'ts.
- Competition mindset.

Choosing a competition that's right for YOU...

If you've not been climbing long, then turning up at the World Sport Climbing Championships is likely to end in disappointment. In general, the bigger the competition, the higher the stakes. So, if you decide to enter a regional, national, or international competition, you will be competing against seasoned athletes, often who are part of a coached 'squad', and who will probably have years of climbing experience. Rules will be rigorously enforced and the attendees probably more serious. It shouldn't put you off – there are plenty of climbers who rise through the ranks without formal training - but appreciating this should help manage your expectations.

Local competitions are a great place to start. Plenty of climbing gyms run their own competitions, with multiple problems to try. As there is likely to be a rich diversity of competitors, from absolute novices to professional climbers, you can approach it exactly how YOU want to - with the attitude that you're just going to have some fun or, much more seriously, competing to win.

Whichever route you choose, you are much more likely to enjoy the experience if you are prepared...

Ready or not?! - Pre-competition essentials

Pack your climbing gear

Seriously, the last thing you'll want to be doing is running around on the day of the competition searching for your shoes, or discovering your favourite climbing trousers are in the washing machine. Gather everything you mean to use, wear, or take the day before your competition. Start with the most important items:

1. *Climbing shoes*

and

2. *Chalk*

And then also consider packing:

3. *A pen*

Yeah, I appreciate it's the 20th Century, but believe me, the day you don't bring one is the day you spot your favourite celeb and neither of you have got a pen! Pack one! You may need it to sign a waiver, physically record your score, or simply write some useful notes.

4. *Cash*

Invariably at one time or another, the single, 1980's, 'made-in-Kurdistan' card payment machine at the climbing gym will go down. Suddenly everyone's scrabbling for loose change! Save yourself time and energy by bringing enough money to cover car parking and emergency snacks. A stack of loose coinage in the car will also come in useful for car parking machines.

5. *Repair kit*

So, when I say "repair kit", I mean a "BODY repair kit". I could have said, "Bring a first aid kit," but that sounds bad, and I might as well have just said, "Be prepared to injure yourself!"

Truth is, you're probably going to try and climb harder than ever before. That's GREAT NEWS, although it also means you're more likely to push your body to the limit... and when you push your body to the limit, the possibility of injury increases. So, just pack a repair kit - Okay! Okay! Mini first aid kit - with contents that will enable you to treat minor injuries. I'm not talking about a medical bag equipped for brain surgery… there are just a few things worth carrying in case of one of several common climbing afflictions:

a.   *Sterile tape*

A FLAPPER isn't just someone who gets excitable in a stressful situation, it's the colloquial term for a torn or ripped piece of skin that is just sort of hanging there… flapping! Grabbing hold, after hold, after hold can be tough on the skin, particularly your finger pads. Occasionally the skin may split. It's hardly life threatening but it can be painful. Continuing to climb untreated isn't a great idea, because the skin is likely to tear more, and the soft new skin underneath really needs time to harden up.

Besides, you essentially have an open wound which is like a MAGIC PORTAL FOR GERMS to get inside your body. LOTS and LOTS and LOTS of people will have gripped the holds that you're about to put your open wound on and, I guarantee, some of them won't have washed their hands. Add to that the fact that some holds will have been stepped on with climbing shoes - perhaps the same climbing shoes that have been worn in the toilet block - and you can see how it's possible to get a revolting infection! So, protect torn or sensitive skin and try and prevent nasty germs getting in wounds, by ensuring you have some STERILE TAPE.

"You might want to put some tape on that!"

Tape is also good for finger joints that are sore, having been put under additional pressure on hard competition climbs…

Although it's not so good for gripping holds, so balance how much you need it and apply accordingly.

b.   *Skin file*

Useful to rub down calluses and file away dead skin, but please remember to dispose of it hygienically (e.g. in a bin rather than on the floor, in your mouth, or over your lunch).

c.   *Nail scissors / clippers*

Avoid long fingernails: they make a horrible clawing noise on the holds, and worse still, can snap or rip. Well-manicured fingernails are going to find it easier to grip even the tiniest crimps.

Also, avoid long toenails – they can be excruciating, squashed into the front of a climbing shoe. Better to keep them trim so that your shoe fits snugly around your toes. And it goes without saying - dispose of nails hygienically too!

d.   *Cold pack & compression bandages*

A STRAIN of a muscle or tendon, or SPRAIN of a ligament, is a relatively common injury in any sport. The commonly acknowledged initial treatment of such soft tissue injury is 'RICE'. No… don't go packing your local supermarket's easy cook sweet and sour rice; I am referring to the mnemonic for treatment:

- **REST** - essential to allow the body time to repair.

- **ICE** - application to the injured area reduces inflammation and pain.

- **COMPRESSION** - a compression bandage can help reduce swelling.

- **ELEVATION** - lift the limb, which also helps to reduce swelling.

So, another couple of useful items in the repair kit are COLD PACKS (e.g. an instant chemical icepack) and COMPRESSION BANDAGES (e.g. an elastic bandage or compression sleeve), both of which are cheap, easy to use, and can be instantly applied to injured areas by yourself, or with the help of a friend or dedicated first aider. Any good climbing gym should already have these to hand, but it's worth packing your own just in case.

It is worth highlighting that whilst RICE is often advocated in the short-term, many experts suggest that after an initial period of rest, movement of the injured area and heat can actually be better in the longer-term. Consider consulting a health care professional for personalised advice.

6.   *Drinks (Exchange the 'de' for 're' - hydrated)*

If you've been climbing hard or the temperature is high, your body produces sweat to regulate its temperature. The sweat cools your body down as it evaporates from the skin. Men and women have an average of two to four million sweat glands… That's a lot of sweat! And, as sweat is mostly water, all that fluid needs replacing.

YOU MUST DRINK at regular intervals, rather than just when you become thirsty. If you FEEL THIRSTY it is more than likely you are already DEHYDRATED. Mental and physical performance suffers with even the slightest levels of dehydration. So, before you climb, HYDRATE, and then during climbing, HYDRATE!

What's that... You don't like water?

Throw me a bone here!

How can you NOT like water?!

You are literally made of it!!!

The average adult human is approximately 55-60% water.

If you can't stomach normal water, then consider packing coconut water, which naturally replaces electrolytes lost through sweat, or enough flavoured hydration/isotonic drinks for the day. Oral rehydration salts may also help reduce your likelihood of becoming a HUMAN RAISIN.

"Human raisin?" "You'd shrivel up 'like a raisin' with no fluid in your body"

"Oh yeah, GRAPE example!"

As your focus during a competition is likely to be elsewhere - such as climbing at maximum effort, possibly within a time limit - consider setting a reminder on your watch or phone for a drink.

7. Grub... lots of grub

Most climbing gyms will have a café/tuck shop selling exorbitantly priced chocolate, cereal and energy bars, cakes (YUM), and an assortment of standard paninis and sandwiches, ranging from DARN TASTY to DAMN RIGHT DEPLORABLE. Even if the climbing gym boasts a 5-star gourmet restaurant, I advise taking your own packed lunch, as typically there will be a massive queue at the one time you should be climbing / watching your loved one climb, or the card machine has broken (see CASH)! You need to have adequate provisions to provide the sustained level of energy that is required for an all day/half day outing.

Don't risk getting HANGRY!

It is true of cars, as it is your body - you need to put the right fuel in to obtain the best performance. Stuff it full of fries, a dirty burger, slice of pepperoni pizza, all washed down with a litre of fizzy soda and, although you may feel satisfied, you may as well have loaded a couple of pounds of salt and sugar in your underpants for all the good it will do in improving your competitive edge!

Ideally, you want to graze at regular intervals throughout the day, on foods that steadily release fuel into the bloodstream.

So, pack healthy sources of carbohydrate, the rocket fuel of athletes, such as: whole grain cereal bars, granola, or a pot of dried fruit or pasta.

Also munch nuts and seeds because you'd like to be like a tiny squirrel – num num num - nibbling away, OR because they pack an ALMIGHTY amount of energy.

And love them or hate them, bung in a banana. When you need a quick snack, these bad boys are packed full of energy and seratonin (fabulous for enhancing mood), although, bear in mind that if they're anything like EVERY BANANA EVER, they're bound to get squashed to mulch unless you wrap them up as snug as a baby in swaddling.

8. *Camera (optional)*

If you've got a phone, chances are it will have a camera, but just consider: if your loved one is clamouring to new heights or on the podium in their moment of glory, they'll want a NATIONAL GEOGRAPHIC WINNER PIC taken of them. Chances are your phone does some great selfie shots, but over an arms-length and snaps are going to start looking grainy. And that's without anyone moving... So, if you have a half decent camera, bring it along!

Prepare for action! - How to prepare for the competition

It's easy to forget the simplest things when you're under pressure... things you suddenly discover when it's too late - like the journey to the competition takes twice as long as anticipated. So, even once you've gathered all your climbing gear together, make sure you have planned for your up-and-coming event:

Catch some Zzzzzzzzz's

The night before a climbing competition is NOT the time to complete a back-to-back film marathon, dance your socks off at a late-night club, or try and beat the impossible end of level monsters on your gaming system. Scientific experiment has proven that, not only does sleep play a restorative function, but improved length and quality of sleep is linked to improved performance and competitive success. So, get counting sheep!

Wakey, wakey, eggs and bacey... Breakfast choice

EAT ONE! Preferably a healthy, nutritious meal. A small bowl of sugar encrusted cereal or a breakfast biscuit is not going to be sufficient. You need to FUEL THE MACHINE (that's you BTW).

Stuffing yourself to the brim 5 minutes before the competition starts is equally unlikely to help you reach your full potential. So, whatever you choose, leave yourself an hour or two to allow your body to digest it!

Rules of engagement - Know the comp rules!

If you're lucky, the rules for a competition will be posted online, or sent out after you've completed an entry form. Make sure you read them. Some things will be obvious, but other elements may be less so and worthy of note. Examples include:

- You are only likely to have a limited number of attempts at a route.

- If you're preparing to climb - LOOK, DON'T TOUCH until you are ready to start your ascent - touching a hold could be classed as an attempt.

- You're not allowed to use holds from another route to help your ascent.

- Marking on the edge of a boulder problem, often by a strip of black tape, means you can't use anything the other side of it for your ascent.

- You may have limited time to complete a route.

- You mustn't squirt oil on other competitors' shoes.

If there aren't any published rules, judges should explain the format before proceedings commence. If they don't, ASK during registration and, failing that, ask someone who looks like they know what they're doing (although avoid anyone likely to be your climbing competition evil arch-enemy).

It's a long way to Tipperary! - Journey planning

If your chosen competition is at your local climbing gym, then you should roughly know how long it will take to get there, but plan for delay: temporary road works, the car won't start, or a freak meteorological event. Travelling further afield may require a little more thought. Make sure you know exactly which route to take, be it by foot, car, bus, train, tram, plane, boat, or horse-drawn carriage.

If you are travelling by public transport, then check that there aren't any scheduled timetable changes. If you have your own transport, then consider that a lot of climbing gyms are located within industrial estates, with insufficient parking for the increased numbers expected at a competition. Generally, it's going to be first come, first served. I've witnessed some competitors sleeping in their vehicles overnight to guarantee a spot. I guess it depends on how keen/bonkers you are...

As much as there might be spaces outside other businesses not linked to the climbing gym, often unscrupulous car parking companies will jump on the opportunity to stick a penalty notice on your vehicle. Suddenly your parking charge is more than a meal for two at a swanky restaurant. It pays to do a bit of research on the cheapest nearby parking. Besides, a brisk walk is likely to do you good and help disperse any nerves.

Always have a plan B.

And don't forget to plan your route back home...

Timeliness

Get to the climbing gym early. When I say "early", early is NOT 5 minutes before the start... I mean an hour early; at least. You've got to find your way around, potentially register, anxiously chat to people you recognise as well as some you don't, look at the climbing routes (if you're allowed), go to the toilet for a nervous wee (at least every 2 minutes), and finally, WARM UP.

Battle tactics - Competition do's and don'ts...

When you arrive

1. **Confirm that you are registered for the competition.** Some climbing gyms may open to normal climbing, with a competition running in an apportioned area. If the registration point is different to the reception desk, head straight there and get signed in.

   Confirm you are in the right age category, the start time, and EXACTLY where you need to be to begin. This is especially important in competitions where there is a defined starting order. If you're not in the right place at the right time in such a situation, you could miss your go altogether!

   "Something ain't quite right here!"

2. **Establish how your score will be recorded** (Hopefully, this will have been clear when you'd read the rules – HINT HINT!). Often, you will be given a SCORECARD, a slip of paper numbered with each route which will be used to record your score after each climb. Sometimes there will be a judge on each problem who will record your score, and sometimes there won't, in which case you must record your own score (HONESTLY!). Whichever method it is, guard the scorecard with your LIFE! It won't be a very satisfying experience if you FLASH (achieve on your first go) 8 out of 8 routes only to realise you have no proof whatsoever! Alternatively, the competition organisers may rely on a phone app with the scorecard accessed electronically. If so, download the app as soon as possible, remembering that some apps can take AGES to download, particularly if there is a sudden influx of users (e.g. everyone at the start of a competition).

3. **Locate the toilets** - you're going to need them, and you certainly don't want to be 'caught short' if there's a big queue.

4. **IF YOU ARE ALLOWED, go and study the routes.** This will allow you to mentally prepare for what is ahead. If the order of the routes isn't set (i.e. you choose your own order), then note down which ones you believe will be EASY, HARD, or MEDIUM. When the competition finally starts, you should consider mixing the order that you attempt each of the categorised climbs. For example: 1 x MEDIUM, followed by 2 x EASY, followed by 1 x HARD, etc. Leaving all of the hardest climbs until last may not be prudent as this is likely to be when you are most tired.

5. **Plan the order of your routes**: Given the choice, it's common for nearly EVERYONE to try and dive on the easiest climb. Starting with easier climbs is a great way of calming your nerves, but try not to wait too long. The more people that have mauled the holds, the more they can become sweaty and greasy (mmmmm, greasy holds), making the route more difficult to climb. Alternatively, you could avoid the crowds from the word, "GO!" and instead consider starting on a harder route. After all, you should have warmed up (please say you've warmed up!), and you're going to have to give it a go at some point anyway.

When you are ready to climb

"I'm not taking any chances!"

6. Don't be afraid to **brush the holds** within reach. But remember - don't clamber on the route to do so - it could be counted as your climb!

7. **Nail the climbs that suit your style**. It's a great way of building your confidence, getting some points on the board, and gives you time to concentrate on the ones that are going to be more of a 'project'.

6. **Realise** that you will always score zero on the climbs you don't attempt. Give all the climbs a go. You may surprise yourself!

9. **Take your time to look at the route**: from the very bottom to the very top, and consider how you would ascend it, planning for contingencies. If a hold isn't as good as it looks from the ground, do you have a Plan B... Plan C?

10. **Make every hold count**. Climbing competitions are often won or lost on very small margins:

    Most bouldering competitions include a ZONE HOLD – a hold along the route – that if reached, will provide the climber with a score. The zone is useful because, even if you have no chance of reaching the final hold or 'TOP' (for maximum points), you can still aim to get some points on your scorecard. Competitions are often won or lost on the difference of a zone hold, so literally grab it if you can!

    Similarly, in rope climbing competitions, if you attempt to reach a hold but fail, you may still be awarded an extra mark (usually a plus +) for the attempt itself (e.g. Climber A got to hold 23, purposefully moved towards hold 24 before falling and was awarded 23+, as opposed to Climber B who simply dropped off hold 23).

When you finish a route

11. If you reach the final hold and there is a judge, **turn and look at them** (if you're physically capable of doing so!). This is your moment of glory, and you want to be assured they have recorded it.

12. Similarly, if a judge is marking your score card, **check straight away that they have marked it correctly**. There's nothing worse than topping a route only to realise 20 minutes later the judge didn't record it, missed a signature, or ticked the wrong box. A single absent mark could mean the difference between a podium... or not.

Throughout the competition

13. **Queue-time is not the time to be daydreaming**. USE THIS TIME to:

    (a) Rehydrate.

    (b) Wolf down some high energy snacks.

    (c) Stretch, loosen, or keep your joints warm.

    (d) Watch other climbers: What techniques do they use to ascend the climb? What bits will you imitate? What bits will you avoid?

    "I should very much like to avoid the falling off bit..."

14. **Forget about the climb you've just done** (or not done!) or the one you're going to do later... they don't matter a jot... FOCUS on what is in front of you.

15. **Try not to fixate on solving one problem**. Some routes may be so difficult that no one will be able to do them. If you concentrate on one climb more than others, you may miss out on the points available on more achievable routes.

16. **If you find yourself stuck, go and climb something else**. It will give your mind and body time to rest and recalibrate. Sometimes you will find that after a short break, a climb that has thwarted you, suddenly becomes climbable.

17. **Support and encourage fellow competitors**. It makes for a much more fun environment, and others will reciprocate, giving a welcome boost in your time of need!

18. **Use available time constructively**. It can be nice to watch good climbers, catch up with your buddies, and cheer people on, but also make sure you leave enough time for the actual climbing. Even if there isn't a time limit, you want to ensure you give yourself the best competitive chance by climbing when you are still fresh.

Some competitions use an ISOLATION format for the qualification, semi-final, or final. Climbers are segregated in an area where they are unable to see the next route or watch others climb it. Each climb will instead be a MAGICAL MYSTERY TOUR. But before the magic starts, each climber must wait patiently until it is their turn. Depending on the number of competitors, this can be nerve-wracking and/or BORING! If you find yourself in this situation, listen to music, read a book, or write your memoirs, but make sure you know when you're likely to begin because you also want to use your time to warm-up, stretch, and focus.

When the competition has ended

19. **Treat yourself**. Eat an ice cream as big as your HEAD, watch your favourite movie, or go out for a meal with your climbing buddies. Not only do you deserve it, but it is good to end on the day on a positive (however you feel you did in the competition).

One last point on mindset...

How would you eat an elephant? Well, hopefully you wouldn't... for starters, they're one of the most majestic animals on the planet, and secondly, I suspect it would be like eating an old shoe. The point is, if you DID eat an elephant, you wouldn't eat it in one go - it would be a huge and impossible task. You should eat it in small mouthfuls! In the same vein, don't be overwhelmed by the competition as a whole. With all the nervous energy, it's easy to feel like it's all TOO MUCH!

Accept the fact that you will feel nervous. Everyone does. It's just some people don't admit it!

Realise that if you have followed the advice in this chapter, you've already broken things down into tiny bite-sized morsels, so you needn't worry about:

- Having had a good night sleep.
- Eating an adequate breakfast.
- Knowing the rules.
- Parking.
- Having your climbing gear, a pen, camera, cash, and repair kit.
- Getting there on time.
- Having sufficient food and drink.
- Going to the toilet.
- Registering.
- Your competition tactics.

These are all the areas that YOU can **influence** and **control**. Getting these areas sorted will automatically reduce your stress and allow you to concentrate on the actual climbing.

Conversely, you have NO INFLUENCE over:

- The organisation of the competition.
- The difficulty of the routes.
- The ability of other competitors.

So don't waste an iota of your time or energy thinking about them!

Also remember that on the day, whilst you cannot suddenly radically alter your general technique, strength, or flexibility, you can however seek to ensure you have the right MINDSET. So, accept that you may feel anxious and focus on positive self-talk.

Sometimes competitions are emotional affairs. Climbers can put immense pressure on themselves to do well. And often the adage, "It's the taking part that counts," doesn't always sink in. But remember, if you aim to climb a mountain, occasionally you will stumble, but it shouldn't stop you from one day getting to the top.

The least you need to know

- Concentrate on what you can influence, such as having had a good night's sleep, eating an adequate breakfast, parking, having your climbing gear, a pen, camera, cash, and repair kit, getting to the competition on time, registering and establishing the format, rules, and scoring, having sufficient food and drink, going to the toilet, registration, checking the routes, and warming up.

- Use your time to read your routes, watch other climbers, and keeping yourself warm, hydrated, and fuelled.

- Identify if a route is hard, medium, or easy and have a strategy for the order in which you attempt them. Don't fixate on one route, try them all. If you can't reach the top hold, try and secure the highest (for ropes) or zone hold (for bouldering), to harvest as many points as possible.

- Don't waste any time worrying about issues you can't influence, such as the organisation of the competition, difficulty of the routes, or the ability of other competitors.

- Smile. It takes physical and mental strength to enter a competition. You should be proud of yourself.

(My wife always has...) THE FINAL WORD

So, you've got to the end of the book... hopefully by reading it.

I hope you found it valuable, either as an aid to climbing, or as a door wedge, fly splatter, or means of balancing an unsteady table.

A cautionary word:

Just after you popped out of the womb, could you run? Could you cartwheel, stand on one leg, or do a handstand? I'm going to hazard a guess of "NO!" So, I'm going to be straight with you – after reading this book you're not going to be ready to trad climb 1000 metres up the notorious El Capitan either. Not even if you read it twice because it was the only book you'd packed to go on a long flight and there wasn't a TV... or Wi-Fi... and you hadn't downloaded any movies to your phone... and particularly because I didn't cover multi-pitch trad climbing...

H-O-W-E-V-E-R... it will provide you with an understanding of the core skills essential for any climb. Apply this knowledge to help achieve whatever goal you set.

So, flick back to the relevant sections whenever you need them, maybe read another book, watch a few videos, but in the main... CLIMB!

See you on the wall.

ACKNOWLEDGEMENTS

- My wife, Laura, for ~~putting up with me~~ her unwavering support, acquiescing to my career break to write this book, and not insisting I tidy the house every day because I'm "not actually working". And, of course, for always being there for me, from the darkest hour to the brightest day.

- My daughters, Amelie and Florence, for their love of climbing, pushing me to try and reach their standard (and failing miserably), posing for and then laughing at my awful drawings.

- My father, Peter, a non-climber, for his honest review of my scribblings and for surviving his heart attack, at least long enough to see the book published!

- My mother, Rosemary, a non-climber, for supporting my desire to write, saving my father, and ultimately for creating me.

- My friend, GB Climbing Coach and Oakwood Head Climbing Coach Jon Redshaw, for his time and dedication in reviewing the completed manuscript, adding his unique and qualified insight, and ensuring the content is technically sound. His intricate knowledge of the subject, combined with his calm and positive coaching style has enabled many, many athletes to achieve their aspirations.

- My climbing buddy, Mat Hearn, for dedicating an inordinate amount of his own time to provide an honest review of the first draft. He applied logic and order to a piece of work that would otherwise be a rambling collection of climbing facts (although I anticipate some might argue it still is).

- My friend, illustrator Zac Freeman, for their patience and guidance in teaching me how to transform my pathetic pencil doodles into a digital artform (or into pathetic digital doodles depending on your perspective).

- My climbing buddy, Owen Hayward, for calling upon knowledge from a former lifetime as a graphic designer and teaching me to apply it to the collection of text and pictures I had amassed, to form an actual book.

- My friends, performance climbing coaches Guy Davenport and Robin O'Leary, for selecting my daughters for Oakwood Youth Climbing Squad and launching our family into the world of competitive climbing. Their continued coaching expertise and infectious enthusiasm for the sport helped awaken my own thirst for knowledge and passion for climbing.

- Charity Oakwood Youth Challenge, for supporting the formation of a parent run, not-for-profit climbing squad, enabling the development of talented young climbers.

- The family dogs, Mable and Olive, for leaving my pristine new Apple pencil for a whole week before chewing the end to a fine mulch whilst somehow missing any essential components, and thereby allowing me to use it to draw the illustrations.

APPENDIX A

Approximate conversion chart of commonly used BOULDERING grade systems in Europe & the USA

V-SCALE or HUECO SCALE		FONT SCALE (Fb)
VB	Beginners...	3
V0		4
V1		5
V2	Intermediate, including the majority of climbers on the planet...	5+
V3		6A/6A+
V4		6B/6B+
V5		6C/6C+
V6	Expert, dedicated climbers...	6C+/7A
V7		7A+
V8		7B/7B+
V9		7B+/7C
V10		7C+
V11	Professional climbers, lizards, monkeys, and spiders...	8A
V12		8A+
V13		8B
V14		8B+
V15		8C
V16	Superhumans and bizarre alien lifeforms...	8C+
V17		9A

Note: The Font scale originates from a region of France often credited as the birthplace of bouldering... Fontainebleau. Try not to mix this up with the other French grade system - the French Sport Grade System, used for rope climbs (see Appendix B!).

APPENDIX B

Approximate conversion chart of commonly used sport climbing grade systems in Europe & the USA

FRENCH SPORT SYSTEM	YOSEMITE DECIMAL SYSTEM (YDS)
3	5.4
4a	5.5
4b	5.6
4c	5.7
5a	5.8
5b	5.9
5c	5.10a
6a	5.10b
6a+	5.10c
6b	5.10d
6b+	5.11a
6c	5.11b
6c+	5.11c
7a	5.11d
7a+	5.12a
7b	5.12b
7b+	5.12c
7c	5.12d
7c+	5.13a
8a	5.13b
8a+	5.13c
8b	5.13d
8b+	5.14a
8c	5.14b
8c+	5.14c
9a	5.14d
9a+	5.15a
9b	5.15b
9b+	5.15c
9c	5.15d

Getting to grips

OOO... you have been practising!

Serious dedication required

Whoa! People are going to stop and watch your incredible feats of human endurance...

Are you of this world?

INDEX

A

Adaptive climbers 15
Anchor 11, 82
Automatic belay 98-100

B

Bat hang 76
Belayer, Belaying 85-97
Belay device 87
Belay loop 105-106
Bouldering 8, 33-40, 122-128, 167-170
Boulder mat 118, 122-123
Brake 88-90
Breathing 54, 154-155
Bridging 73
Buddy checks 85, 92-93

C

Cave 42
Centre of gravity 63-65
Chalk 22-25
Chalk bags 24
Chimneying 72
Cold water shock 133-134
Communication 95-97
Competitions 159-172
Crack climbing 125-127
Crimp 44

D

Dead rope 89
Deep water soloing 10, 129-135
Disco leg 60
Down climbing 36, 139
Drop knee 73
Dynamic movement 66-68
Dynamic rope 107
Dyno 68-69

E

Edging 57
Exposure 123

F

Falling 37-38, 97, 134-135, 152-155
Finger jam 126
Fist jam 126
Flagging 65-66
Flexibility 146-150
Foot hold 46, 57-59
Foot jam 127
Footwork 56-62
Free solo 10

G

Gaston 44
Gear loops 105-106
Grades 34-36, 94-95, 133
Guidebook 117, 131

H

Hand jam 126
Harness 105-107
Heel hook 75-76
Helmets 101-105
Holds 43-49

I

Ice climbing 13
Indoor climbing gym 26

J

Jug 43

K

Karabiner 87-88
Knee bar 74
Knots 82-84

L

Layback 71-72
Lead climbing 11
Leg loops 105-106
Lock-off 77
Lowering 90

M

Mantling, Mantelshelfing 77-79
Mindset 52, 151-155, 171-172

N

O

Overhang 42
Outdoor climbing 112-128

P

Pocket 45
Pinch 45
Precision 52, 56
Psicobloc 10, 129-135

Q

R

Rockover 65
Rope 107-111

S

S-scale 133
Scorecard 167
Shoes 17-21
Side pull 44
Single rope 108-110
Slab 41,
Slack 94, 97
Slipping 61-62
Sloper 43
Smearing 59-60
Speed climbing 12
Spotter, spotting 39, 122-123
Static climbing 66-68
Strength training 140-145

T

Tides 132
Tie in loops 105-106
Toe hooks 75-76
Top rope 10, 80-98
Trad climbing 11
Tying in 82- 85
Types of climbing 8

U

Undercut 45

V

V-scale 35-36
Visualisation 155-156
Volume 46

W

Wall angles 41-43
Warm ups 30-32
Weight differential 91-92

X

Y

Z

Zone hold 168

Printed in Great Britain
by Amazon